Ulster Coastal Run
A Running and Sometimes Walking Adventure Around the Northern Coastline

To John & Carmel,

Hope you enjoy the book and you learn something new and get visit some of these places

Gerry

ORLA KELLY
PUBLISHING

Gerry O'Boyle

Photo credit: County Donegal Map - Wesley Johnson

Published in Ireland by Orla Kelly Publishing.

'Sand for the feet of
the runner'

Oscar Wilde

*This book is dedicated to my son Brian who is a student at Clifton Special School in Bangor, Co. Down.
All profits go to Clifton School.*

Brian on Chapel Island, Strangford Lough (Stage 6, Revisited)

Contents

❖

Coasting around Ulster (The Clifton Coastal Run)

"I always loved running. It was something you could do by yourself and under your own power. You could go in any direction, fast or slow as you wanted, fighting the wind if you felt like it, seeking out new sights just on the strength of your feet and the courage of your lungs." Jesse Owens

Welcome to my story. Whether you're a reader or a runner (or both), I will try to keep this fun and interesting. So, as you read this, please try to keep up with me. I promise not to go too fast! This adventure started on Saturday 11 February 2017 in Omeath, Co. Louth (just south of the Ulster border). By running only once a month, I completed the whole coast of Ulster and arrived in Bundoran on 15 September 2019. That's a total of 1,590 km or 988 miles.

I suppose I've always had an adventurous spirit inside me just waiting to escape! Even when I was seven or eight growing up in Rahoon Road, Galway City I often wondered what was beyond the green fields outside the town. I remember thinking how far you could go before you could get lost! As I got older, I realised you had to go further and further if you really wanted to lose yourself to a particular place or to a certain moment. The real answer to the question –"how far do you have to go to get lost", is probably Donegal. I know because I've taken so many wrong turns in that county! At that particular time when I'm looking at my map, I'm not thinking of, what happened yesterday, or what might happen tomorrow. I'm completely lost in that moment. There's a certain excitement in not knowing where exactly you are – alone in the wilderness and trying to figure out the best option to take. Getting lost is an essential part of the whole adventure!

Whose idea was this anyway?

I must admit I've had this idea of a Coastal Run for a long time. Then one of my comrades, at North Down Athletic Club, Terry Eakin, actually stole this idea –my idea! Well, that's not technically true. As I hadn't actually told anyone about my plan, I can't really accuse someone of stealing my idea. Terry decided himself in 2013 that he was going to run the whole coast of Northern Ireland – and he did complete it and ran all the way around the coast of Northern Ireland in the calendar year of 2013. Terry told me that he enjoyed his coastal run much more than any race or event that he had ever completed in his life. I understood completely what he meant, and this made me envy Terry's adventure even more. I was also secretly determined to follow in his footsteps, but I still kept the idea to myself, until October 2016. On one weekend on 8/9 October 2016, I happened to mention the coastal run idea (in two separate conversations) to both Helen Byers and Sean Nickell, and they were both very interested and even enthusiastic about a coastal run. I knew then I had found two similar mad accomplices, and suddenly, the Clifton Coastal Run was born!

My son Brian and Clifton Special School

This adventure is called 'Clifton Coastal Run' after Clifton Special School (a school for children with learning difficulties in Bangor, Co. Down). My wife Maureen and I moved to Bangor in 1996, and my son Brian has been attending Clifton School since he was five years old. Maureen gave birth to our beautiful son in March 2004, and Brian was a wee brother to our three older boys. He was born with a cleft pallet (a gap on the back of his mouth) and had difficulties at the beginning with his feeding and had to spend the first few weeks in hospital in a special care unit. A doctor at Belfast Royal hospital explained to us what a cleft pallet was and how it happened. It seemed that, as Brian's body was forming in the womb, parts of his mouth did not come together properly; so poor Brian had to have an operation when he was eight months old. This procedure turned out to be very successful, and the gap in his pallet was closed. At this stage, Brian was babbling like a normal baby, and as he came to his first birthday, he even took his first steps. However, as the months went by, we realised that Brian was developing much slower in other areas. Anyway, to make a long story short, Brian was then diagnosed with autism and 'severe learning difficulties'. Looking back now, I think that, like his cleft pallet, his brain never came together properly. Despite his problems, Brian has grown into such a happy boy and has a lovely warm personality. Those of you who are reading this and have had the pleasure of meeting Brian, will now be nodding in agreement! Physically Brian has no real issues. Later, you will see that he has even joined me (walking) on quite a few of my coastal adventures, climbing some tough hills in Donegal and crossing over causeways to remote islands on Strangford Lough. I tried to get him into running, but he doesn't see the point in it, like a lot of people. Brian loves his school, and happily hops onto his yellow bus every morning. Since Brian's first year, I have been involved with the PTA at Clifton School and have helped raise funds over the years. Special needs children have special (and unique) requirements which can be complicated and expensive to satisfy. Clifton School always needs IT equipment and other specialised tools for children with disabilities. So thank you so much for buying this book and playing your part in helping our school. And if you haven't run with me so far, maybe you'll join me as I continue my run around the rest of Ireland. *See blog to read the continuing story at* **https://cliftoncoastalrun.blogspot.com**

Places and History

This book isn't just about running. It combines my love of running with my love of history, people, stories and places. I think I've also inherited my father's interest in people. At my father's funeral, the priest said my Dad had a 'countryman's curiosity'. My father always wanted to make some connection with everyone, and perhaps it's an Irish thing. We always want to know the background of a person or place. The Dublin author James Plunkett wrote what was probably my favourite book, Strumpet City, which has eleven different characters connected to each other in some way. Plunkett also published a beautiful travel diary called "The Gems She Wore". His book is a lovely casual trip around Ireland, and the writer talks about various places and historical events in a matter-of-fact kind of way. So, like James Plunkett, I'm trying to bring a similar casual conversational interest about famous places that I've been to. At times I did really feel a sense of history as I passed through various towns, villages, harbours and beaches. On this adventure, I've learned so much more about my adopted province.

The perfect team for our adventure

I know I was so lucky to have found the two most perfect partners for this adventure. I got to know Helen and Sean through North Down Athletic Club (NDAC), and I know I could never have accomplished this run without these two warriors, even if they did leave me to complete Co. Donegal on my own.

Sean was raring to go from the beginning! If the truth be told, Sean Nickell could probably do the whole Co. Down coast in one day or at least in a weekend. He's competed in lots of ultra-marathons and is regularly one of the last one standing in these events! Sean also has a son in Clifton Special School – that wee boy Conor with the cutest smile – so this adventure is close to Sean's heart too.

Helen Byers was equally passionate about the whole experience and such a determined runner who always pushes herself to the limit. I got to know Helen first through our teaching and accounting careers, and she's become such a good friend over the years. She has a few sub 3.30 marathons under her belt too, and if you want to run a parkrun inside a prison, Helen is the person who will get you in! (see Stage 15)

I was so privileged that Helen and Sean joined me. The three of us completed all of the coast of Northern Ireland together, having the best of craic along the way. Unfortunately (for me) it was difficult for Sean and Helen to continue into Donegal. The three of us all had day-jobs (and young children), and at times it was tough trying to squeeze our runs into a suitable weekend. So I continued on my own into Donegal and tackled its long, meandering coastline. However, I was delighted that Helen and Sean did return to join me again during a magical weekend in July 2019. We stayed in a remote hostel in Malinbeg (near Glencolmcille) in the south-west corner of Donegal and enjoyed some lovely weather. We climbed the cliffs of Slieve League, running across 'one man's pass' and had the perfect celebration afterwards in the Rusty Mackerel in Teelin.

Apart from Helen and Sean quite a few other members of NDAC have joined me along the way. On the Donaghadee to Belfast stage, there were ten runners from NDAC with me! One of the best decisions I made in life (apart from marrying my wife Maureen) was to join NDAC. I've met so many great people over the years and have made lasting friendships. So if you're reading this and you've run with me, thank you so much – you made it so much easier. If you haven't run with me yet, you can still join me as I move further south along the Irish coast.

It was March 2018 when Helen, Sean and I finally completed all of Northern Ireland. I felt at that stage, with the weather getting better, that I might as well continue into Donegal. I suppose I had another reason to keep running. I wanted to complete the proper Ulster coast. Without getting too political, I always preferred treating Ulster's province as an entity rather than the state of Northern Ireland. Some people reading this might not even know that Ulster also includes Monaghan, Cavan and Donegal. I often thought that it was a shame that Ulster's traditional and ancient province was split in two when

Northern Ireland was created in 1921. Donegal probably suffered most because of this arrangement, cut off from Derry and Belfast by a border and too far away from Dublin for the Irish government to care. When we stayed in the lovely wee hostel in Malinbeg, the owner, Frank expressed these sentiments as well and told us that Donegal was the 'forgotten county'. Well, I'll never forget my amazing journey, up and down those rolling hills and along its spectacular coastline.

In the actual recording of this adventure, I was lucky to have Sean and Helen with me for the Northern Ireland section. Helen took some lovely pictures, and they were both quite meticulous in recording the mileage and posting it up on Strava and our Clifton Coastal Blog. Until I reached Donegal, I didn't even have a stop watch, and so I had to purchase a Garmin watch and educate myself about uploading my runs onto Strava. Except for one small section in Donegal (Kinnagoe Beach to Culdaff) I've been able to post all my coastal runs onto Strava and onto my blog. I like to see that wee map of where I've been especially when I circle a peninsula or tidal island (by the way on Strava I'm Gerry Jarlath O'Boyle)

In this book, I've tried to record my coastal journey to make it easy for someone following in my footsteps. I've even gone into more details in my blog, describing every path and turn I've taken. I would encourage everyone to try to tackle some of this beautiful coastline. It might be hard to take on this challenge by just walking the coast, rather than running – on the law of averages it would probably take two or three times as long, but what's the hurry! I suppose most of the adventure could be done on a bike although I would not like to cycle through some of the bog lands or over cliff paths in west Donegal. However each stage of this adventure can be tackled in its own right and remember, there's no time limit or deadline (well, maybe sometimes there's a time limit regarding tides and daylight - as I discovered a few times!)

Sand (and music) for the feet of the runner

It's interesting to look back when we started our adventure at the beginning of 2017. My original plan seemed quite sensible and straightforward. I had planned to run along the County Down's coast in different stages (once a month) over a calendar year. However, Helen and Sean seemed more ambitious and talked about doing all of Northern Ireland. In either case, it seemed sensible to start our run at the Down/Louth border, running south to north, keeping the sea on our right-hand side and strictly following the coast at all times.

Of course, a nice beach along the way (and there were many) helped us stick to our task, which reminds me of what Oscar Wilde said about the Greeks and their attitude to life. Oscar Wilde wrote his famous letter 'De Profundis' from Reading Gaol in1897. (By the way, I lived in Reading for six years in the early nineties and that's where I first started running.) When Oscar Wilde was in Reading Gaol he wasn't allowed to write any novels, short stories or plays but he did have permission to write letters, no matter how long they were, so he composed 'De Profundis', which literally means, 'from the depths' . In his long letter (or essay) from the depths of despair, Oscar obviously misses the outside world and writes.....

"I have a strange longing for the great simple primeval things, such as the sea, to me no less of a mother than the Earth. It seems to me that we all look at Nature too much, and live with her too little. I discern great sanity in the Greek attitude. They never chattered about sunsets, or discussed whether the shadows on the grass were really mauve or not. But they saw that the sea was for the swimmer, and the sand for the feet of the runner".

I always loved Oscar Wilde's phrase '**sand for the feet of the runner**'. I thought of this so often on my adventure and referred to it many times in my coastal blog.

When I'm running along the coast, it's usually free from any traffic noise, with just the seagulls and the sounds of the crashing waves to keep me company. I never wear earphones or listen to music while I'm running. I much prefer the natural sounds of the birds, other wildlife and the wild sea itself. However, I have to admit that every time I'm running on a beach, I can always hear those piano notes from Vangelis' Chariots of Fire. By the way Vangelis was Greek and his own father was an accomplished sprinter. Despite running in sleet and hailstones on Portstewart strand, I could still hear the Chariots of Fire music (in my head!), and I heard those notes again and again on every remote beach in Donegal. Sometimes running on a strand, I even start to hum those six opening bars to myself.... da da da da da da. In 2013, I was so lucky to have the pleasure of running on that famous beach in Scotland where the film's opening scenes were shot. My eldest son Conor was living in St Andrews at the time and I went to visit him there. Conor and I had to wait a while for low tide at the West Sands beach, but it was well worth the wait, and yes, it was the perfect sand for the feet of the runner! Maybe the idea for the Coastal Run was forming in my head at that time!

With my son Conor on 'Chariots of Fire' beach in St. Andrews, Scotland

The original plan

This is what I wrote back in my blog in December 2016, referring only to Co. Down.

"The southern part of County Down (where we'll start) is dominated completely by the amazing and majestic Mountains of Mourne and as per the song; the mountains actually do 'sweep down to the sea.' So for the first part of our journey, we'll have the sea on our right-hand side and the mountains on our left. Strange to think that if someone took this journey a thousand years ago, they'd have the same two running companions as we'll have'.

Then there's the 'Van Morrison section' around Ardglass, made famous in his song 'Coney Island'. (Actually Van's song isn't really a song – more of a poem, really - and Coney Island isn't really an island!). When we reach Strangford, we'll take the much longer route (via Newtownards) to Portaferry."

Well, that was my original plan – to run only the coast of Co. Down - but as you see we ended up running around all of Northern Ireland and in addition to that, I carried on running around the whole coast of Co. Donegal. Of course, after completing the Ulster coast I couldn't resist the challenge of running around the entire coast of Ireland.

Like the great Jessie Owens, I always loved running, and for this difficult task, I always felt so privileged to have my health, fitness and energy. I never took it for granted that I had been given the opportunity to see so many beautiful and spectacular places along the way. More than anything else, I know I'm lucky to have such good friends and family to support me. I know I'm even more fortunate to have my best friend (and long-suffering wife!), Maureen, who is so understanding and patient with me, allowing me to tackle this crazy adventure.

Places I Revisited:

You will notice in reading my story, stage by stage, that I sometimes add **Places I Revisited** onto a section. As I was running along the coast, I tried to stick rigidly with the shoreline as far as possible, but sometimes, I didn't reach every corner of the coast for various reasons. However, if that happened, I try to go back to complete the bit I missed! I joke that I'm always afraid that the 'Coastal Audit Committee' will check up on me but to be honest it does bother me a little if I miss a section of the coast. I just have to go back to complete it! It also gave me a chance to take my son Brian with me, and after all, this whole adventure is dedicated to him and Clifton School. Brian has been such a good companion on these unusual Sunday afternoon trips, although I did have to make sure I had an adequate food supply for our picnics!

So what or where were the places I revisited? I missed Fair Head on Co. Antrim in January 2017 as the road to the cliffs was covered in ice, and it was too treacherous to run on. In September 2018, I missed Melmore Head in Donegal after taking a silly wrong turn in the Rossguill Peninsula. I ran out of daylight in September 2019 on my way to Rossnowlagh – that bit I was able to complete the following morning. However, the most common reason for not completing a section was because of high tides – there was either no beach to run on, or the causeway to a tidal island was covered.

The islands of Ulster

During my coastal run, I developed a particular interest in the islands around our shores, especially those ones you can reach at low tide. I've always been fascinated by tides and how the whole landscape changes with the tides each day; and this happens twice a day, every day! Growing up in Galway city and living only about 2 km from the beach at Salthill, we were always aware of the tides. Salthill always looked so much better at high tide; you had nice sand to paddle in, and the natural swimming pools filled up. In Bangor where I live now, I'm only 1 km from Ballyholme beach, and the tide will still influence me in deciding when to go for a walk or run. When I was planning my coastal adventures, I did my best to match them with low tides, but that wasn't easy at times. Nearly all the runs were on Saturday mornings, so I had to accept the tide as it was.

However, sometimes I had to go back and revisit a section. When I did go back I planned my return paying particular attention to the tides. All the islands (below) were reached without getting on a boat! You should always check the tides before attempting to reach any island. Remember the sailors 'rule of twelfths'; the tide comes in very slowly in the first hour (1/12), but it moves twice as fast in the second hour (2/12) and three times as fast in the third hour (3/12). My advice is to cross over to any tidal island about two hours before low tide, although every island is different.

In my whole adventure, I got to cover sixteen different islands. When I did return to complete a stage, I was lucky that a few of these tidal islands that I missed were on Strangford Lough (a salty sea inlet), which is close to where I live in Bangor. This meant I had more time to complete the task, and sometimes I took my son Brian along, and we were able to walk around the islands. It's not always about running, you know!

The sixteen islands I ran (or walked) around were as follows:

- Sketrick Island, Co. Down: Yes, not much of an island but it has a pub, called Daft Eddies which Helen, Sean and I were very glad to visit on a warm June day (See Stage 5)

- Reagh & Mahee Islands, Co. Down: I reached these islands on a cold but beautiful December morning with a group of my Sunday Morning runners (See Stage 5)

- Island Hill, Co. Down: Brian (his first island) and I walked across the causeway on a mild November day (See Stage 6)

- Gores Island, Co. Down: Another causeway that Brian and I crossed on a brisk November afternoon (See Stage 5)

- Mid Island, South Island and Chapel Island, Co. Down: Brian and I were joined by one of my other sons, Matthew on a beautiful May morning (See Stage 6)

- Inch Island, Co. Donegal: My friend Johnny McGrath accompanied me in running around this large island on a mild January morning (See Stage 19)

- Island Roy, Co. Donegal: Did this one on my own on the Rosguill peninsula on a pleasant October morning (See Stage 24)

- Cruit Island, Co. Donegal: Another one I reached on my own on a mild March day (See Stage 28)

- Inish Caoil, Co. Donegal: I ran around this tidal island after arriving in Portnoo with Valerie & Philip McDonough on a sunny May afternoon (See Stage 31)

- Ernan's Island: This was just outside Donegal town, and I arrived there on a lovely September evening. (See Stage 38)

- Oilean na Marbh (the island of the dead), Co. Donegal. Maureen and Brian joined me on a showery December afternoon (See Stage 28)

- Gibbs Island, Co. Down: My sons Daniel and Brian accompanied me on a sunny December day (See Stage 5)

- Friend Island, Groomsport, Co. Down: Maureen and I walked to this island from our home in Bangor at sunrise one May morning. (see Stage 8)

And of course I never needed to get on a boat to reach any of those sixteen islands! I should mention that I also covered three more 'islands', which can't really be classed as islands.

- Co. Antrim's Islandmagee which is just a large peninsula (See Stage 9)

- Co. Donegal's Doagh Isle was once an island but over the years the channel between the island and mainland has silted up. The Irish Open Golf Championship was held on Ballyliffin golf course on Doagh in 2018. (See Stage 17)

- Co. Down's Coney Island which isn't really an island (made famous by Van Morrison of course.) I should point out that there is another Coney Island in Co. Sligo and there is no doubt about it being an island; it's 2.5 km from the mainland and a most beautiful Atlantic isle. Since covering the coast of Ulster, I've continued running around the rest of Ireland and on a beautiful day in September 2020 my wife Maureen and son Brian walked across in our bare feet (at low tide) to Coney Island, Co. Sligo. You'll have to read my blog (**https://cliftoncoastalrun. blogspot.com**) for more detail about that. (Stage 44)

Although this Island is not in Ulster, it's the original Coney Island

Then there were a few other small islands that I couldn't get to for various reasons – mostly because they seemed to be in private ownership.

- Castle Island West, just north of Killyleagh, Co. Down: Brian and I drove to Ringhaddy Pier and began to walk along a lane heading north to the island. A scary barking dog stopped us in our tracks and then a couple came out of their house explaining politely that we would need some kind of code or key from the National Trust to access Castle Island. We never went back!

- Hare Island, just south of Killyleagh, Co. Down: Brian and I tried to reach this island from both sides of Strangford Lough. From the east side, we tried to access it from Castle Island (east) road. We could only get as far as Quoile Yacht Club where there were 'no entry' signs. Then, there didn't seem to be any road or lane to Hare Island from the west side. We also tried walking from Gibbs Island, but it got quite rough, and it looked as if you would have to go through someone's back garden to reach it!

- Rolly Island and Cross Island, east of Comber, Co. Down: I passed near these islands (See Stage 6) with my Sunday Morning Running Group as the winter sun was coming up over Strangford Lough. We were on our way to Mahee Island and ancient Nendrum. Both these islands were clearly marked 'Private'.

- Feehary Island, Shamrock Island and Conly Island, just south of Whiterock, Co. Down: There was a narrow lane up a hill leading towards Feehary island, but again more 'Private Road' signs along the way. It looked like Shamrock Island, and Conly Island could be reached at low tide, but you would have to access another private lane and probably walk across some muddy fields after that. We didn't get to any of these three islands.

- Guns Island, north of Ardglass, Co. Down: I passed this island twice, once with Helen and Sean and then again at low tide on a summers day with my son, Brian. Even at low tide, this didn't look accessible at all, and there was no causeway to the island. (See Stage 4)

- Inishinny Island, Carrickfin, Co. Donegal: I dragged Maureen and Brian back here on a fairly miserable December day. This island is right at the top of Carrickfin peninsula and east of the more famous Gola Island (Dimigh go Gabhla). At low tide, there was a great expanse of sand from the mainland, so we made our way across. However, just before we reached Inishinny itself, there was a wide water channel that made it impossible to reach the island. (See also Stage 28)

- Island Ravedy, Melmore Head, Co. Donegal: This is one that got away! I had planned to go back at low tide, but with so many restrictions and lockdowns I never made back to NW Donegal. It looks like there is no road or lane to this island so I'm not even sure if I could have made it there anyway. I read that there is a Lighthouse on the island and that you should be careful crossing as the tide can cover the causeway.

As I continue my run into Connacht, I think I'm going to try to reach a few more tidal islands. I'll make sure to stick to two rules: It has to be safe, and I have to reach the island without getting on a boat!

January 2017 – one month before Start

"The will to win means nothing if you haven't the will to prepare"
Juma Ikangaa

This is what I wrote just one month before our start. *"Our long coastal journey will start next month, and we're counting down the days to 11 February 2017. Helen and Sean are equally excited about our task ahead. The t-shirts with the Clifton School logo arrive just before Christmas. The three of us all run the parkrun on Christmas Eve in Bangor, and afterwards we arrange to head down to nearby Ballyholme beach for a few pictures wearing our new bright lime green shirts. I'm excited about our crazy idea! At my age, it's probably the closest I'll ever get to a proper adventure. I almost feel a little like Ernest Shackleton going on an arctic expedition – I suppose we all have an adventurous spirit hidden somewhere inside us"*

I've always admired Shackleton and how he looked after his men on those ambitious adventures. It's still not clear if he ever did put that advert in the Times Newspaper (Men wanted for hazardous journey; low wages, bitter cold, long hours of complete darkness, safe return doubtful) but if I lived a hundred years ago I probably would have answered his call and joined him on his ship, the Endurance.

In January 2017, the local newspaper (County Down Spectator) did a small piece about our forthcoming run. The paper's artist (Neal McCullough from Hand Drawn Creative) does quite a funny sketch of the three of us, even if he refers to us as *'Joggers'* in his cartoon!

"There's no going back now", Sean says!

Cartoon in newspaper before our adventure begins

The Coastal team on home soil (Ballyholme Beach, Bangor, Co. Down)

Visiting Omeath, Co. Louth (where Coastal Run begins)

On Sunday 15 January 2017, Maureen, Brian and I decide to head down to Omeath where our Coastal Run will start in a few weeks. Where exactly is Omeath, you might ask? Omeath is a small village in County Louth, just south of the border – about halfway between Carlingford and Newry. It's a beautiful January day when we arrive in the village and Warrenpoint and Rostrevor can be clearly seen, nestling in the Mournes across the bay.

In Omeath, I get talking to a couple of runners (not joggers!). They're going for a run in the opposite direction, towards Carlingford. The old railway line from Omeath to Carlingford is now converted into a lovely coastal greenway, perfect for running, walking or cycling but the path seems to stop at Omeath. I tell these runners about our coastal run idea and enquire about the best way to go from Omeath to Newry. I had already read that the old railway line went as far as Newry, but I wasn't sure whether that section was suitable for running yet. One of the men said we should come back next year (2018) when the greenway from Omeath to Newry would be finished!

Anyway, on this beautiful day in mid-January, Maureen and I leave Omeath and drive across the border back in towards Newry and around the river/canal towards Rostrevor, with the sea and Cooley Mountains on one side and the Mournes on the other. Of course, this is the area that inspired CS Lewis when writing the Chronicles of Narnia. In a letter to his brother, he wrote

> *"that part of Rostrevor which overlooks Carlingford Lough,*
> *is my idea of Narnia"*

Yes, you can see why he was so impressed, and I was hoping we would get as good a day for the start of our Coastal Run next month in February 2017.

January 2017 - one month before start of Coastal Run, Omeath, Co. Louth

Coast of Ulster – Stage by Stage

Stages	Month	Start	Finish		km	Miles
1	Feb-17	Omeath	Rosstrevor	along Newry canal & via Newry City	26.5	16.5
2	Mar-17	Rosstrevor	Kilkeel	via Warrenpoint and Cranfield beach	26.8	16.7
3	Apr-17	Kilkeel	Dundrum	via Moore Road & shore to Annalong	35.1	21.8
4	May-17	Dundrum	Strangford	via Ardglass & St John's Point Lighthouse	43.0	26.7
4	Aug-20	*Revisited*		Ballyhornan to Nature Reserve, near Kilclief	4.0	2.5
5	Jun-17	Strangford	Comber	via Castle Ward, Saul, Delamont &Daft Eddies	57.5	35.7
5	Nov-19	*Revisited*		To complete circle of Gores Island	9.6	6.0
5	Dec-19	*Revisited*		Islands of Reagh & Mahee + ancient Nendrum	10.4	6.5
5	Dec-20	*Revisited*		Gibbs Island - no extra mileage		
6	Jul-17	Comber	Portaferry	via Flood Gates (N'Ards) and via Abbacy Road	40.0	24.9
6	Nov-19	*Revisited*		To Island Hill/Rough Island near Comber	5.6	3.5
6	May-20	*Revisited*		Mid Island, South Island & Chapel Island	10.3	6.4
7	Aug-17	Portaferry	Donaghadee	Via Ballyquinton Point at bottom of Ards	53.0	32.9
8	Sept-17	Donaghadee	Belfast	via Coastal Path & Bangor parkrun	40.0	24.9
8	May-20	*Revisited*		Friend Island - no extra mileage		
9	Oct-17	Belfast	Islandmagee	via Gobbins Road on Islandmagee	39.9	24.8
9	Dec-20	*Revisited*		The Gobbins - no extra mileage		
10	Nov-17	Islandmagee	Larne	via Ballycarry & Glenoe Waterfall	43.0	26.7
11	Dec-17	Larne	Cushendall	via Glenarm, Carnlough and Waterfoot	35.9	22.3
12	Jan-18	Cushendall	Ballycastle	Via Cushendun Coast rd & Torr Head	31.0	19.3
12	Jun-20	*Revisited*		*To Murlough Bay and Fair Head*	10.3	6.4
13	Feb-18	Ballycastle	Portrush	via Rope Bridge & Giants Causeway	40.0	25.0
14	Feb-18	Portrush	Benone	via Portstewart strand & Castlerock	42.0	26.0
15	Mar-18	Benone	Muff	via Magilligan Prison & Bellarena	55.0	34.2
15	Jul-20	*Revisited*		Via shoreline & Ballykelly bank – No extra miles!		
16	Apr-18	Muff	Culdaff	via Inishowen Head & Kinnagoe Beach	56.0	34.8
17	May-18	Culdaff	Ballyliffen	via Malin Head, Malin town and Doagh Isle	69.8	43.4
18	May-18	Ballyliffen	Buncrana	via Tullagh Point, Dunaff & Mamore Gap	36.5	22.7
19	Jun-18	Buncrana	Letterkenny	via Inch Island and Grange Causeway	51.2	31.8
19	Jan-19	*Revisited*		To complete full circle of Inch Island	11.6	7.2
20	Jun-18	Letterkenny	Portsalon	via Ballylin Point, Ramelton & Rathmullen	50.6	31.4
21	July-18	Portsalon	Fanad Lodge	via Fanad Head & Lighthouse	21.4	13.3

22	Aug-18	Fanad Lodge	Fanad Lodge	full circle of NW coast of Fanad peninsula	35.4	22.0
23	Aug-18	Fanad Lodge	Carrickart	via Carrowkeel, Millford & Cranford	39.2	24.3
24	Sep-18	Carrickart	Creeslough	via Island Roy, Tra na Rosann & Downings	39.9	24.8
24	Oct-18	*Revisited*		*To top of Melmore Hd on Rosguill*	9.6	6.0
25	Oct-18	Creeslough	Dunfanaghy	via Ards Forest, Marble Hill & Horn Head	44.8	27.8
26	Jan-19	Dunfanaghy	Falcarragh	via Tra Mor & Falcarragh Beach	29.2	18.2
27	Mar-19	Falcarragh	Bunbeg	via Bloody Foreland & Gaoth Dobhair	40.8	25.3
28	Mar-19	Bunbeg	Dungloe	via Donegal Airport & Cruit Island	58.2	36.1
29	May-19	Dungloe	Meenacross	via Termon & Falcorrib Coast road	23.3	14.4
30	May-19	Meenacross	Dooey Point	via Drom Loch Druid	15.5	9.6
31	May-19	Dooey Point	Portnoo	via Dooey Strand Beach & Inis Caoil Island	25.9	16.1
32	Jun-19	Portnoo	Ardara	via Dunmore Hill and to Loughros Point	42.3	26.3
33	Jul-19	Ardara	Glencolmcille	via Assarnacally Waterfall & Glen River	31.5	19.5
34	Jul-19	Glencolmcille	Teelin	via MalinBeg, Sl.League & One man's Pass	26.6	16.5
35	Jul-19	Teelin	Killybegs	via Carrick, Kilcar and Muckross Point	26.0	16.2
36	Aug-19	Killybegs	St Johns Point	via Drumanoo Hd. & Carntullagh Hd.	35.4	22.0
37	Aug-19	St John's Point	Donegal town	via Inver village, Doorin Point & Salthill	44.3	27.5
38	Sep-19	Donegal Town	Rossnowlagh	via Ernan's island & Donegal Golf course	26.9	16.7
39	Sep-19	Rossnowlagh	Ballyshannon	via Creevy Pier and Creevy Coastal Path	22.3	13.9
40	Sep-19	Ballyshannon	Bundoran	via Tullan Strand & Bundoran Cliff path	17.3	10.7

Total distance covered around coast of Ulster 1,590 988

km   Miles

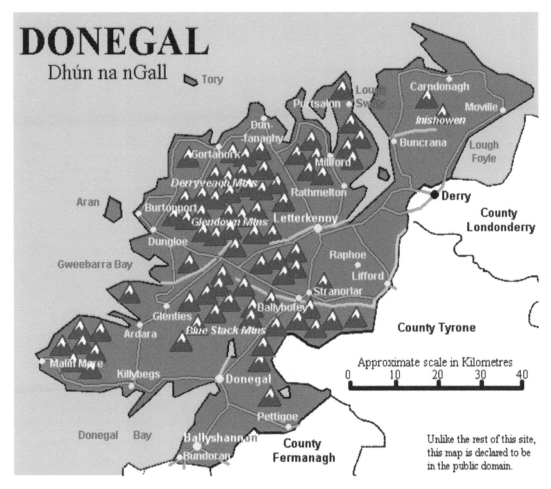

Photo credit: Kind permission from Wesley Johnston

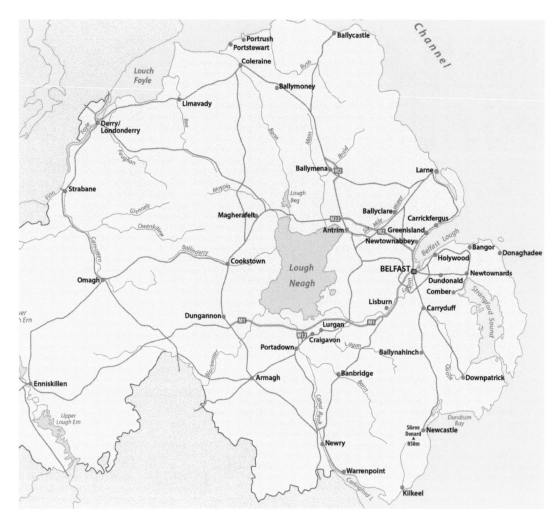

Map of Northern Ireland

STAGE 1:

— ❖ —

Omeath (Co. Louth) to Rostrevor (Co. Down)

Date: 11th February 2017

26.5 km or 16.5 miles

"All great deeds and all great thoughts have a ridiculous beginning." Albert Camus

Helen, Sean and I started our grand coastal adventure just south of the Co. Down/ Co. Louth border. Looking across the river/sea from Omeath, we could already see today's finish line on the other side at Rostrevor, Co. Down.

It was an early start and a nice spring morning (I'm going by the old Celtic calendar that says spring starts on 1st Feb) as we headed for Rostrevor. Helen and Sean decide to run the Kilbroney parkrun in Rostrevor first. However I decide to rest as I've picked up a back injury in the last few weeks and decide to save my energy for the main event! Well, after all, I am the elder on this adventure.

After the parkrun with Helen and Sean barely out of breath, I drive the three of us the 16 miles to Omeath, leaving Sean's car in Rostrevor.

.........and so at last, our adventure began in Omeath, Co. Louth at exactly 11.05am on Sat 11 Feb 2017 ......and this mad idea isn't just an idea anymore. It's now really happening!

The snow started to come down as we started our run, but it soon faded away, although still very cold. As we run along the road from Omeath to Newry looking across at the beautiful

Mournes (the area which inspired CS Lewis's and the Chronicles of Narnia), I can't help thinking about a horrific event that took place in 1979. (The same day Lord Mountbatten was murdered by the IRA) On that August day, 18 soldiers were killed by the IRA at Warrenpoint, just across the narrow river from Omeath. Another victim of that day was a curious English tourist (on the Omeath side of the river) who was shot dead by British soldiers in the mistaken belief he was one of the bombers who detonated the bomb.

Back in a much more peaceful 2017, we continue running along towards Newry and eventually cross over from Co. Louth to Co. Down. (the border). All the talk in the news recently after the Brexit vote last summer is about what kind of border we will have. Well, there's definitely no sign of a hard border here! In fact, there's no real sign of any kind of a border as we cross over from the Republic into Northern Ireland.

As we arrive at the quays in Newry, we decide to stop off for a takeaway coffee before heading towards Warrenpoint. Just outside Newry, we find a grassy path overlooking the river and enjoy running along this traffic-free ridge for a few miles. Eventually, however the path comes to an end and we have to join the Newry-Warrenpoint dual carriageway. It's a busy road here but relatively safe on the footpath.

Our first stop at 'the Quays' in Newry

After a while, I suggest (bad idea in hindsight!) that there is another easier way closer to the river and it would be much nicer to run along this path. Now we're struggling through fields and find ourselves trapped between the river and a wee stream. We see a man, and we start to worry that it's his field we're trampling on. We ask him for directions. He suggests we carry on through the field (it wasn't his land anyway). "Keep going" he says, *"until you reach thon house"* as he pointed in the distance. Eventually we somehow find our way back out onto the dual carriageway, at the aforementioned 'thon house'

We strolled through Warrenpoint, and we picked up speed again as we got on the Rostrevor road. This was a much better and quieter stretch with the river widening on our right-hand side and a lovely feeling that we were now definitely in the heart of the Mournes.

As we get closer to Rostrevor, Helen is pulling away, leaving a wide gap between her and Sean and me. To slow her down we suggest we stop at the big monument erected in memory of General Robert Ross. We climb up the path and steep steps to the top of the monument (with lovely view across the bay) and read all about the famous General Ross.

He will forever be remembered as the man who burned down the White House! The 'Burning of Washington' took place in 1814, during the War between British forces and the USA. One eyewitness testified that General Ross was personally involved in the piling up of furniture and kindling for the White House, preparing to destroy the landmark. It was the only time that a foreign power captured and occupied Washington. (And unbelievably just recently in January 2021 Trump supporters invaded the Capitol in Washington and almost did a similar job to their own capital city!)

View across the bay to Cooley Mountains from Ross's Monument, Rosstrevor, Co. Down

The rain is coming down now, but we don't care! Now it's just a short run to our finish point in Rostrevor. It's such a great feeling, completing that first leg of our journey and we couldn't have picked a nicer place to end our first run than Rostrevor, nestling in the Mournes. CS Lewis wasn't the only one who was impressed with this area. The famous English writer, Thackeray also wrote *'were such a bay lying upon an English shores, it would be a world's wonder and travellers would flock to it'*

STAGE 2:

❖

Co. Down: Rostrevor to Kilkeel (via Cranfield)

Saturday 11 March 2017

26.8 km or 16.7 miles

"You can't be miserable when you're running. It's such a simple and pure way to feel alive." Veronica Rossi, Brooke

A lovely new movie La La Land is making all the headlines at the moment, but we were back down to CS Lewis' 'Narnia Land' in Rostrevor to complete the second stage of our coastal run. Now it's spring and a little warmer than last month. It was even an earlier start this time, leaving Bangor in two different cars at 6.45am and driving down through the majestic, but hazy Mourne Mountains.

There were six of us today. Three new runners joined us, Colin Walker, Chris Stevenson and Michael Stevenson. Colin is probably the main reason you notice many more people running in the North Down area, mainly through his 'New Beginnings' group. Chris has been running a while, has done a few long runs in his time and completed a few marathons. Michael (no relation to Chris) is a relatively new member of NDAC, but he's become an expert at long-distance runs and has even done a few ultra marathons.

We started where we finished last month in the beautiful Kilbroney Park in Rostrevor. Everyone, except me (still recovering from injury), decides to do the parkrun at Kilbroney – and really, you couldn't get a nicer setting for it.

The Holm oak tree, Rostrevor - Northern Ireland's 'tree of the year'

Yes I can't believe I'm struggling with this hip injury on only the second stage of this great adventure! Still I'm determined to keep going and I decide to save my energy by walking on ahead of the others. I arrange to meet everyone else about an hour later at the castle in Greencastle. It was quiet enough on the main road towards Kilkeel, but in any case, I was lucky enough to have a footpath to walk on nearly all of the way. After about 6 miles, there's a right turn towards Greencastle and Cranfield, heading south on a quieter country road. After about half a mile I come across 'Eileen's Store', my last chance for refreshments before I get to Kilkeel. Eileen and her husband John are so friendly, making me a cup of coffee but refusing to take any money for it.

I carry on walking alone; crossing the bridge over the White Water River and then take a right towards Greencastle. There used to be a ferry here going over to Greenore in Co. Louth (just over a mile across the bay) but the ferry hasn't gone since 1951. Apparently, the first ferry was in 1185 between the two castles of Carlingford and Greencastle. There's talk recently about running it again, but local opinion seems to be against it. 'NO Ferry Here', says a big sign nearby. I think the locals are worried about too much traffic in their area. Just a few months after we completed our run, the ferry restarted again.

I walk up the hill to the actual castle itself at Greencastle, one of the oldest castles in Ireland, built almost 800 years ago, in 1230 by Hugh de Lacy. It's now mid-day, the sun is threatening to shine, and soon I see in the distance the rest of the coastal runners coming along. The sheep in the fields nearby are bleating like crazy now at the sight of these strange people.

The castle at Greencastle, Co. Down

During World War 2, a special aerodrome was built here in Greencastle, Co. Down, which became home for the US Army soldiers in preparation for the D-Day operation in Normandy. General Patton even came here to check his troops – he called his soldiers, the *'fittest, readiest outfit that I've ever inspected'*. I'm sure he would have said something similar if he had seen today's six coastal runners!

Leaving Greencastle, we now do a U-turn, back the way we came. I decide to start running for the first time today (after my long walk from Rosstrevor). We take a right turn along Fair Road. This road is called Fair Road because Greencastle was once the 'Capital of the Mourne Kingdom' and its fairs were the most famous in all of Ulster. Fair Road leads down towards the sea, and after a while, we then find ourselves on the west side of Cranfield beach.

On Cranfield beach, Co. Down (re-enacting the cartoon by Neal McCullough)

We are reminded again in Cranfield beach about a horrible disaster that took place on 3 November 1916 (we had seen another monument about this at the Quays in Newry last month). During a terrible storm, two ships (SS Connemara and Retriever) collided, killing 94 people. James Boyle, a non-swimmer, was the only survivor but refused to ever speak about this incident until he was an old man. Even the 34ft high Haulbowline lighthouse in the bay couldn't stop a disaster like this happening. Strange that today the sea was so smooth and calm and it was hard to imagine this happening.

It's still quite a high tide when we get to the east side of Cranfield, and we're wondering whether we should run around the corner on the shore or take the country road back towards Kilkeel. We send Sean on a mission to discover whether it's feasible to run along the beach. We wait and wait and eventually, positive news comes by text from Sean – *'yes it's safe to go along the beach'*. We all run along the shore, sometimes struggling among the rocks, and eventually we find a path that leads off the beach, onto a narrow lane and back onto the country road to our finish line in Kilkeel. I was glad to run part of the way today, and I hope to feel a bit better for our next run in April. Stage 2 completed!

STAGE 3:

— ❖ —

Co. Down: Kilkeel to Dundrum

Saturday 1 April 2017

35.1 km or 21.8 miles

"Running- if there's any activity happier, more exhilarating, more nourishing to the imagination, I can't think what it might be." Joyce Oates

It was just Helen, Sean and me today. We're back to the Mourne Mountains again to the wee fishing harbour in Kilkeel to start stage three of our journey. I must admit that we were a little apprehensive about today's stage of our adventure. Those of you who know the Kilkeel-Newcastle road will notice that it's a busy, twisty road and doesn't always have a footpath alongside it. We always try to take the scenic route, but on this occasion, there isn't really a proper coastal path, and it's mostly rocky shoreline. To make our task even more difficult today, the forecast was for some heavy showers. Also with my hip injury still playing up, I've hardly done any running since the last coastal run.

We left Bangor at 6.45am, hoping that a low tide at 9.10 might help us. We parked again at the Leisure Centre, near Kilkeel harbour. As we are getting ready for today's adventure, Mrs. Graham (Helen's friend's Mum) kindly came to wish us luck, giving us a donation towards Clifton School. Thank you Tracey's Mum!

We run towards Kilkeel town centre, continuing along the Newcastle Road for about half a mile until we came to a crossroads at Moor Road and then take a right turn, running down towards the coast again. For a while, we have a grassy trail or a flat enough pebbly beach to run on. There are spectacular views here on both sides, inland across the Mournes, with Slieve Binnian towering in the distance and then on our right-hand side the calm Irish Sea. The sun was shining too and no sign of any showers on the way!

However, as we get closer to Ballymartin the terrain is getting worst, more rocks than pebbles on the beach now and adding to that, swarms of flies confront us. Sean said they were Mayflies – not sure about that and anyway it's only April! I read that, in Ballymartin in 1858, a Spanish boat sailing from Liverpool to Barcelona went off course (slightly!) and hit the rocks. The impact was so severe that it split a huge stone in two and since then the stone in Ballymartin has been called Barcelona Rock.

We keep running/walking along the rocky shore, although there is a small sandy beach near Ballymartin. We're stepping over more rocks now, but we notice a trail slightly inland as we get closer to Annalong. This is definitely easier on the feet. We arrive in Annalong harbour and talk to a lady called Maureen Scott who is out walking with her dog, Bell. When she hears our story she generously gives a donation to Clifton School. Thank you Maureen and thank you to everyone who has donated.

Sean and I in the Mournes

We continue north towards Newcastle staying by the shoreline. For the first mile, north of Annalong, there's a rough trail which eventually disappears and we end up running through stones and rocks again. At one stage we find it easier to climb into a farmer's field and run on the long grass, but after a while, even the green fields disappear, and now it's just a rocky shore. The good news is the sun is still shining and no sign of any rain. We can just about make out the Isle of Man in the distance.

The rocks on the shore are getting bigger now, and we realise that we need to go inland. We spot a farmer's gate/entrance near the beach, which leads to a narrow hilly lane inland and eventually we arrive back on the main Kilkeel-Newcastle road about 2 miles south of Bloody Bridge. As we run along the main road heading towards Newcastle, the Mournes are beginning to tower over us on the left-hand side. Helen says she's getting thirsty, but we know we need to keep going until Bloody Bridge.

Helen quenching her thirst at Bloody Bridge (foot of the Mournes)

The Bloody Bridge is exactly where the Mountains of Mourne *'sweep down to the sea'* (as the Percy French song goes). Although we are at sea level, we're only 2 miles from the top of Slieve Donard (higher than any other mountain in either Ulster or Connacht and standing at 852 metres or 2,795 feet). I once did a race where you had to run to the top of Donard and back down again. My claim to fame is that I reached the peak in "less minutes than my age" (it took me 48 minutes 41 seconds to reach the top from sea level and I was 49 years old at the time)

Bloody Bridge

I did a little research on where the name Bloody Bridge came from, and I think it's safe to say that the name goes way back to 1641 when there was an Irish/Catholic uprising in Ulster against the recent protestant planters from Scotland/England. The story goes that there was a massacre here and bodies were thrown into the river, tainting it with blood. I discovered that there were 19,010 pages of recordings of testimonials taken in 1641 (and, believe it or not, these testimonials are still held in Trinity College, Dublin). The best example I could find was a testimonial from Mrs. Crooker recorded in 1641, which is typical of these kinds of killings.

"Elizabeth Crooker was stripped & had taken from her in leather and other household goods; that she herselfe and her son were taken by the Rebells & carried out to the sea to be drowned, others were carried to Newcastle to be hanged."

According to our Ordnance Survey map, there seems to be some kind of coastal trail from Bloody Bridge to Newcastle. However, we realise this is not true, unless we want to follow the same fate as the fictitious character Maggie who fell into the sea near this spot (now called Maggie's Leap). So we continue running along the busy main road again. However, after about a mile, as we get closer to Newcastle, there's a footpath which leads us to the main promenade.

"where dark Mourne sweeps down to the sea"

I'm so relieved to finally arrive in Newcastle. It's been very hard work today and has taken us 3.5 hours to get from Kilkeel. Helen and Sean have been very supportive of me, but my hip hasn't been as sore as I thought it would. We stop for takeaway coffees and stroll along the esplanade and eventually pass the magnificent Slieve Donard hotel which has the most beautiful setting by the sea with the Mourne Mountains facing it.

At this stage, the tide is coming in, but not too far in to stop us running along the coast. We still have another 10 km to run before we get to Dundrum. The Royal Co. Down golf course and sand-dunes are on our left as we continue along the shore. We run along the sandy beach and follow the coast all the way to Dundrum Bay as the sand gets softer and softer, a little too soft for the tired feet of the runner, and I'm really struggling!

At Dundrum Bay, we circle around Murlough (Ireland's first Nature Reserve), and we can now see Dundrum village across the bay. Eventually we cross Downshire Bridge which brings us right into our finish line in Dundrum. Stage 3 is completed!

PS. Twenty minutes later, we drive back to Kilkeel, when the heavens open and the rain comes down. It's the first shower of the day – lucky escape for us!

STAGE 4:

———— ❖ ————

Co. Down: Dundrum to Strangford

Saturday 13 May 2017

43.0 km or 26.7 miles

"Life (and running) is not all about time but about our experiences along the way." Jen Rhines

The weather had been so dry and sunny over the last two weeks but unfortunately, we weren't so lucky today. It was very dull with a light mist falling and staying with us for most of the morning. Even the Mourne Mountains seemed to have disappeared behind the mist and fog.

There were seven of us running today. We were delighted to be joined at the start in Dundrum by four friends – they are running with us for part of today's journey. My good friend and fellow Galwegian/Bangorian, Gerry Coy (nicknamed Gerry the Duke!) has joined us. Gerry's wife, Shona (the Duchess!) has also volunteered to meet us in Strangford at our finish point and drive us to Dundrum where we begin today's run.

Also we're so happy to have Jill Aicken and Sarah Benton running with us today. I have known Jill and Sarah since I've been involved with NDAC about 7 or 8 years. I'm delighted that Louise Watson is joining us too. Louise also has a child, Bethany in Clifton Special School. Louise is a hardened triathlon athlete and could probably swim around the whole Co. Down coast!

At Dundrum (Co. Down) Gerry describes the route, and almost everyone listens!

We decided it was not a good idea (and not safe) to cross the 'causeway' at Dundrum Bay even if the tide was out. In any case, the old grassy railway line around the bay is perfect for us runners. We were easily able to access the old railway line by staying by the shore and passing the old cottages (Widows Row) on our way. This grassy path was a lovely pleasant start to today's run.

Widows Row

We learned that these cottages were built for wives and children of the 73 fishermen who lost their lives in a great fishing disaster of 1843. A commemoration plaque quotes a poem

> *'The sky was dark; the wind was high and bitter looked that day. When ten stout boats with gallant crews set sail from Dundrum Bay'*

We seem to be reporting on many fishing and sea disasters in this coastal adventure of ours, but I suppose it goes with the territory. We continue running on the old railway line. We can easily imagine the old steam engine and carriages trundling along here with the beautiful bay and Mourne Mountains in sight. The line itself was closed in the early 1950s, but at least the grassy surface is maintained today as a beautiful, peaceful walk or run. It's a wee bit sad leaving the beautiful Mournes behind us, and we'll miss those tall hills as we head north. Those mountains have been our constant companions in our early stages in Feb, March and April. I can remember the first time I came here, about 20 years ago with Maureen and just two children, Conor and Daniel. Arriving in Newcastle on a July afternoon, it was misty and foggy (just like the weather today!) and so we felt slightly cheated at not being able to see those famous Mountains. The following morning there was still mist and rain, but then, very slowly the clouds faded away, the mist disappeared, and suddenly the towering Mournes were there right in front of us. It was well worth the wait!

Anyway, we say goodbye to the Mournes behind us (we can't see them through the mist, but we know they're there!) and continue running along the grassy old railway line. After a few miles and without warning the old railway line comes to an abrupt end, and we struggle through fields and farms until we eventually see a bridge (Blackstaff Bridge) and find the road. We take a right turn towards the village of Ballykinler. We avoid the nearby British Army base (there since 1901) on the coast – we can even hear the practice gunfire, so best not take any risks on this part of our journey!

Shortly we arrive on Tyrella Beach, which is a much safer place for us and with the low tide we can make the most of the expansive beach by running on the sand without getting our feet wet.

Two Gerrys on Dundrum Greenway

Sadly, Gerry Coy, the Duke leaves us at Tyrella and his chauffeur, the Duchess is there to meet him. We can just about make out St. John's Lighthouse in the distance, and that's where we're heading. After a while we debate whether we can stay on the beach – it's getting rough and gravely. We decide we need to go inland a little and find the country road. The weather is improving now, the rain has stopped, and behind us, the Mourne Mountains are reappearing, and we can see clearly Slieve Donard and Commedagh in the distance. The country road narrows to a nice quiet lane, and we finally arrive at St. John's Point Lighthouse.

The Duke and Duchess (aka Gerry & Shona Coy)

St John's Lighthouse, Co. Down

St John's Lighthouse

Apparently you can stay overnight at this lighthouse. Not a bad place to wake up and watch the sun rising over the Irish Sea! In 1846 Brunel's famous SS Great Britain made a navigational error and mistook this lighthouse for the Calf lighthouse on the Isle of Man. (yet another nautical disaster!) More recently in 1950, the writer, Brendan Behan also caused havoc when he was employed to maintain and paint St. John's Point lighthouse (this was his day job). Behan's boss wasn't impressed with his attitude at all and wrote.....

> *"Mr. Behan's language is filthy and he is not amenable to any law or order. Empty stinking milk bottles, articles of food, coal, ashes and other debris litter the floor of the place which is now in a scandalous condition of dirt."*

Brendan Behan described himself as a *'drinker with a writing problem'*, and if I'm not mistaken, he got similar negative reviews from his employer in Donaghadee when he painted the famous lighthouse there! Coincidentally, I met a man last month (called Neville) in Galway who also painted/maintained the lighthouses at St. John's Point and Donaghadee, and he told me he had a copy of that letter sent to Brendan Behan.

The next section of the coastal path from St John's Point to Killough was disappointing with lots of litter on the shoreline and sometimes it was hard to find the actual path along here even though it's supposed to be part of the 'Ulster Way'. It was as if this coastal path was designed about 30 years ago and nobody has really updated the signage, stiles or path. A lot of rubbish might have been blown in from the sea. We were glad to reach the lovely village of Killough eventually.

Killough

The harbour was developed in the 18th century by Michael Ward of Castle Ward (which is just outside Strangford). At that time Mr. Ward also organised the building of an amazing straight road that still runs from Killough right up to the front entrance of Castle Ward. Killough village was originally known as St Anne's Port, and it was the afore mentioned Michael Ward who renamed it Port St. Anne, in honour of his wife. Not a bad birthday or anniversary present to give your other half!

If Brendan Behan had the lighthouse painting contract for Ireland, then Alexander Nimmo seemed to have the Irish contract for building piers. It was Mr. Nimmo who built the new quays and a pier here in Killough. In Galway city, the pier there is still called Nimmo's Pier. (Helen also made the nautical connection to that search for that famous fish, 'Finding Nemo')

We follow the coast road in Killough. It is indeed a nice harbour village, and we can understand why Michael and Anne Ward were attracted to it. We can now see Ardglass on the other side of the bay.

Percy French might have written about the Mournes, but Belfast's Van Morrison wrote and recited his famous 'Coney Island' about this part of the world. We're thinking of Van Morrison's words as we get nearer Ardglass and Coney Island.

"Stop off at Ardglass for a couple of jars of Mussels. On and on, over the hill and the craic is good"

Yes the craic is definitely good for us runners too but not sure if we're going to have those mussels when we get to Ardglass! Before Ardglass, we take a right turn onto Green Road (remember, we're trying to strictly follow the coast). The literal translation of the name Ardglass is 'Green hill/height', and indeed it is quite a climb up the Green Road. At

Ardglass, Jill, Sarah and Louise complete their part of the journey. We have a wee coffee and scone break in Ardglass but don't sit down – we might not get up again!

The gate through the Mournes

Leaving Ardglass, we take the main Strangford road, but after about 1 km we take a right turn at Sheepland Road towards Ardtole (Sean says we're really in the Ardtole of nowhere now!) We continue to follow Sheepland Road veering left until we eventually spot the 'Ulster Way' coastal path sign towards a very narrow path leading towards the coast.

We cover a lot of ground very quickly here on this lovely elevated coastal path. Sean leads the way, and Helen describes him as "***a mountain goat that is unleashed, racing around the hilly seaside over many yellow stiles.***"

Eventually at the village of Ballyhornan, we have to leave the coastal path, but we're still on a very quiet country road, the rain has stopped, and the sun is threatening to come out. I'm struggling now, and after about 22 miles, my legs are suffering. However, Helen and Sean are going well and trying to 'carry' me through the rest of the way, and we finally arrive in the port of Strangford. Before today I've never run more than 15 miles so no wonder my body is aching!

So we've now reached Strangford, and for our next leg (Stage Five on 17 June) we could just simply hop on a ferry to Portaferry and continue our run along the east side of the Ards Peninsula. But NO, we're not going to do that! We're going to run all the way around Strangford Lough (via Killyleagh, Comber, Newtownards and Kircubbin) and add about an extra 60 miles to our journey. As usual, we'll keep the sea, or in this case, Strangford Lough on our right-hand side.

Stage 4 – Revisited: small peninsula just north of Ballyhornan, Co. Down

Saturday 29th August 2020

4 km or 2.5 miles

I think it must have been high tide when Helen, Sean and I passed Ballyhornan on our original Stage 4 run in May 2017. Over three years later in August 2020, it was quite a nice day so I decided I would try and see if I could tackle this small peninsula with my son, Brian. Ballyhornan is a small village just about halfway between Ardglass and Strangford. I knew it was low tide at 3.30 pm, which made it easier. Also I was curious to see if it was possible to cross over to nearby Guns Island. We parked the car at Ballyhornan (about a half a mile before the village) and then headed back northeast towards Killard Point.

Brian on the beach near Ballyhornan, Co. Down

Brian and I had to rough it a little at the beginning, but we were quickly onto another beach (not sure of the name of this beach, maybe Benderg), easily followed the coastline around to the Nature Reserve near Kilclief and eventually came back to the main road again. There was a picnic table here at the perfect spot for us, so Brian and I stopped for a wee break. We then walked along the main road back to our car at Ballyhornan.

Interestingly during World War 2, the RAF built billets (small houses) here for the military who worked at nearby Bishopscourt Air Base. Ballyhornan was quite a busy place even after the war with a cinema, dancehalls and shops.

With Brian on Ballyhornan Beach with Gunns Island behind

It is such a lovely long beach in Ballyhornan and Brian and I headed south along the strand until we were close to Guns Island. Even at low tide, it didn't look accessible to cross over to the island, but at least it satisfied my curiosity. Still it was a pleasant view across, and with all the rain we've had recently, it looked like the perfect green isle in the sea.

Stage 4 now completed in full!

STAGE 5:

❖

Co. Down: Strangford to Comber

Saturday 17th June 2017

57.5 km or 35.7 miles

A good run is like a cup of coffee - I'm much nicer after I've had one.

We started our adventure today in the beautiful morning sunshine in the village of Strangford. In fact, Strangford Lough isn't really a lake – it's a salty sea inlet - the largest sea inlet in the British Isles and we're going to run all the way around it (anyway, it only adds an extra 60 miles to our journey!) The name Strangford comes from the Old Norse word – 'strong fjord', and it's also the original home of King Magnus (bare legs). Magnus would have been very proud this morning to see all the barelegged coastal runners!

Our core team of three (Helen, Sean and I) were delighted to have a few more runners with us today. Simon and Keith joined us later in the day but Jill and Sarah – the first runners to come back again for more – started with us in Strangford. So, it's 'Five go for a wee run' as we set off on a beautiful midsummer's morning. Yes, the weather is perfect and even at 8.00 am the sun is high in the sky and already it feels pleasant at 16 degrees.

The Squeeze Gut in Strangford

We're really enjoying learning about new places as we make our way around the Co. Down coast. Today is no exception, and straight away, we discover a narrow pathway at the very top of Strangford at the end of Castle Street. There is a small gap between the Old Court Office and the last house on the hill, and this gap on the left leads to a narrow walled pathway with low flat grassy steps. It's known as the Squeeze Gut. It was built during the Irish Famine in 1847 to provide employment relief. It was said that the Squeeze Gut was named because farmers used to drive their cattle to the ferry this way and larger beasts had to squeeze through. However, our slim running team had no difficulties squeezing through these narrow walls, although we decided to go single file just in case!

Gerry and Sean attempt to squeeze through the 'Squeeze Gut' at Strangford

We exit from the Squeeze Gut on the other side of Strangford. We're still in a wooded area, and after a while, we see a sign for the 'Ulster Way' which brings us down to a rocky, seaweed shore. Sarah made a point about this coastal adventure that 'you never know what's around the corner, but that's all part of the whole enjoyment'. We stick to the coast and struggle along the muddy shore (there's no proper coastal path here) and eventually we come out onto the main road and soon reach the caravan-park entrance at Castle Ward.

Helen, Jill and Sarah at Castle Ward, Co. Down

Castle Ward is one of my favourite places in Northern Ireland, and I have great memories of being here with my children – we even took my parents and mother-in-law here when they came to visit us in the late 1990s. The house and gardens cover a massive 822 acres and were originally owned for centuries by the Ward family but on the death of the 6th Viscount in 1950's the house was presented to the government (in lieu of death duties and taxes). It's now a National Trust property and was the location of *'Winterfell and the Whispering Wood'* in 'Game of Thrones'. You can even dress up in 'Thrones' character costumes from the show – that might have made a nice photo for our blog, but we didn't really have time today!

Of course our own Sean Nickell is very familiar with Castle Ward. It was here he did his 'Last One Standing' running event. Sean completed an amazing 25 laps over 25 hours recently. I was going to say that Sean knows these trails so well that he could probably do this stretch in his sleep – well, running for 25 hours he probably did do some of it in his sleep!

Eventually we have to leave the beautiful Castle Ward Estate at Audleys Castle, and we head along Audleystown Road for about a mile until we come back on the main (Strangford-Downpatrick) road. Luckily we don't have to stay on the main road for very long. We take a right turn down the narrow Myra Road. The only vehicles on this country road are tractors – all the farmers are saving hay today! Myra Road loops around (we're following the Ulster Way and avoiding the main road) and then we cross over the main road again towards Raholp and Saul. After about a quarter of a mile, we take a right turn at Raholp, and we soon find ourselves in the historic area of Saul. On such a marvellous day like today, Co. Down is in full bloom. Who needs to travel to the Camino de Santiago when we've got this on our doorstep! And we even have the religious experience and tradition here in Saul (Saint Patrick's country).

The church in Saul which is in the area where St. Patrick is alleged to have died

Saint Patrick/Saul

Allegedly, St Patrick died in Saul on 17 March 461 and is buried in nearby Downpatrick. Tradition holds that St Patrick and his companions landed at the Slaney River's mouth, a few miles from here, in 432AD. Patrick encountered Dichu, the local chieftain, who gave him a barn for shelter. After passing through Saul, we continue straight (along Mearne Road) until we come back to the main Strangford-Downpatrick road (we don't go into the town of Downpatrick, even though it's only a mile away). We run along a lovely coastal/river path, and then we make a very sharp turn to the right at the bridge (Bridge over the river Quoile!)

Bridge over the river Quoile (just outside Downpatrick)

Although we're now on the main road towards Killyleagh, it's quite safe as we have a footpath to run on for a mile or two. When we run out of footpath, we continue along the main road (running on the right-hand side of course!). We are glad to reach Delamont Country Park. There are spectacular views here in all directions – views of the small islands in Strangford Lough, across to the Ards Peninsula and the Mourne mountains to the south look stunning. We pause at the tall Strangford Stone erected only recently in 1999 to mark the millennium. To give it a proper name this monument is called a Megalith – it stands 10 metres high and was quarried from a single granite slab in the Mournes.

View of Mournes skyline from Delamont Megalith

Sean at the Megalith explaining how the granite is mined

We continue our run, following the narrow paths towards the shore and trying to find the coastal path to Killyleagh. I'm not sure where we went wrong (and I hold my hand up here–it looked easier on Google maps!), but after running for about 20-30 minutes, we somehow end up back at the entrance to Delamont. So, we're back on the main road again heading for Killyleagh. After about half a mile we take a right turn down Shore Road that takes us to Killyleagh harbour, and we run up Irish street to beautiful Killyleagh castle /archway where Simon Robinson is waiting patiently in the warm sunshine to join us. It's now 11.45, and we've already covered 20 miles today. Simon has kindly bought bottles of lemonade for us all, and we can't thank him enough for his generosity. In this weather, it's just what the doctor ordered!

I know Simon as part of a 'Sunday Morning Running WhatsApp' group. Simon usually takes his lively and friendly dog Otto on our Sunday morning run, and now I'm beginning to wish I had four legs to get me through today. It's warming up now (23 degrees), and we welcome our short break in Killyleagh.

Jill and Sarah leave us at Killyleagh, Co. Down

After a 15 minute rest we sadly (for us!) say goodbye to Jill and Sarah and leave Killyleagh Castle heading NW along Shrigley Road which is just alongside the castle. We take a right turn down Clay Road and continue down Ringdufferin Road towards Strangford Lough. This is where it all went wrong!

Yes, Ringhaddy Road did lead down to the coast, but when we went to take a left turn at the shore there was no coastal path and just a house with a big gate, saying Private Property! (we notice a lot of private/no entry signs in this area). We decided to climb down onto the rocky/muddy shore anyway, took a left and struggled along the muddy/seaweed shore for about half a mile and abruptly come to a fence that says *'private property, tres-passers will be prosecuted'*.

So we now had a dilemma – would we turn back on the shore and run all the way back up Ringhaddy Road or would we chance climbing over the fence and risk being prosecuted (someone mentioned the risk of being shot!). We had a third option which we also tried (well Simon did!) -this was crossing the muddy bay! Although it was low tide, there was still a narrow stretch of water to cross and lots of mud/quicksand. Simon volunteered to cross but soon was deep knee in mud before he'd even got half way!

Simon testing the 'mud crossing' in Strangford

We didn't take Simon's muddy option, but half way back we discovered a small entrance off the shore onto a private lane. The property owners soon confronted us, but Sean quickly defused the situation, explaining what we were doing and the landowners let us continue running on their lane. We quickly joined up with Ballymorran Road until we came to a T junction and then took a right turn towards Whiterock and soon we had reached Sketrick Island and the pub 'Daft Eddies'!

Enjoying our break at Daft Eddies on Strangford Lough

We were now totally exhausted but were delighted to meet two fellow runners (Gavin McDonnell and Keith Gilmore) to complete the last 7 miles into Comber with us. Not only did they welcome us, but they provided us with well-needed fuel (orange juice and snacks) to revive us.

We were very tempted to call it a day here at Daft Eddies but decided to continue our run. I think I must have hit the wall at this stage – and I don't think that pint of shandy in Daft Eddies did me any good either – although Helen's pint seemed to give her even more energy! For the last few miles, my legs were so heavy, so it was walking, running, walking ....with Sean and Helen urging me on, all the way to the finish line in Comber.

Stage 5 – Revisited: Gores Island, Co. Down

Sun 24th Nov 2019

9.6 km or 6 miles

When I originally did Stage 5 with Helen and Sean back in June 2017 it would have been hard to try to match our run with a low tide; otherwise, the island's causeway would have been covered. So, together with my son Brian, we set out to reach this island on a very pleasant Sunday afternoon in November. We decided to WALK today and parked the car on a grassy area just about 3 km north of Downpatrick (on the Strangford road) at Castle Island Road.

We keep walking to the very end of Castle Island Road. There we reached Hare Island but couldn't access it as it's occupied by Quoile Yacht Club and has a 'No Entry' sign. We had no alternative but to turn back. And so we tackled Gores Island. It was about 2.30 pm now, and I knew the low tide was at 3.00 pm, so I felt confident about crossing over. Gores Island can also be called a drowned drumlin, and apparently, these drumlins (or hills) became islands when sea levels dropped as glaciers melted.

Brian just before we crossed onto Gores Island on Strangford Lough

When we crossed the causeway and reached the island itself, we followed a tractor trail on the right-hand side. After about half a mile the track ended at a farm gate with very muddy terrain ahead. We got chatting to a couple who were checking their sheep on the island, and they said it was possible to walk around the coast of the island. It was hard work trying to circle the island! Very muddy and lots of climbing gates and fences (some fences seemed to be electric too!). Brian was so good, but nevertheless I was relieved to get back onto the mainland again. Brian and I then sat on a nearby wall by the river and had a lovely (well deserved!) wee picnic of crisps and (homemade) buns! It was only a short walk back to the car.

Stage 5 – Revisited: Reagh & Mahee Islands, Co. Down

Sun 15th Dec 2019

10.4 km or 6.5 miles

When we originally did Stage 5 we discussed getting to these islands, but it was a very warm June day in 2017. We had already run 50 km up to that point and still had to get to Comber! I always had it on my mind to go back, so I did it just before Christmas 2019. Although Reagh and Mahee are really proper islands (surrounded by water!), a narrow road/bridge crosses over onto both, making the islands very easy to reach at any time. I decided the best way to tackle these islands was to start the run in the nearby village of Lisbane. I asked members of my 'Sunday Morning Running WhatsApp' group if they would join me and they did come along in great numbers (including Helen, who of course joined me on every stage in N.Ireland in 2017 and 2018).

So, fourteen of us met in Lisbane at 8.00 am on a bitterly cold, dark and icy morning. I think it was the offer of a full Ulster breakfast at the Poachers Pocket in Lisbane that sold it to everyone! However, the running had to be done before breakfast! So, we all tucked up and tip-toed through the ice along a country road towards Strangford Lough, sign posted Mahee Island. It was tricky enough at the beginning with ice on the country road – downhill, which made it less safe – but it became much easier as we got close to Strangford Lough. With daylight approaching we continued on the 'main road' and crossed over the bridge at Reagh Island.

The sun is rising as we head towards Mahee Island in Strangford

We kept following the course of the road as it looped around to the right towards Mahee Island. We ran up the hill on the island, and the winter sun greeted us as we reached Nendrum Monastic Site. It was a perfect morning to watch the sunrise on this ancient site! The island takes its name from St Machaoi who set up a monastery on the island in the 5th century. St. Machaoi (pronounced Mahee) was the grandson of Diuchiu, the first person that St. Patrick ever converted.

I was thinking how privileged we were, being able to watch the winter sun come up at this ancient site - just like St. Machaoi welcomed the dawn here .. over 1,500 years ago!

Stage 5 - Revisited: Gibbs Island, just south of Killyleagh, Co. Down.

Sunday 20th December 2020

No extra mileage

Back in June 2017, we should have gone down Island Road (300 metres south of Delamont) from the main Downpatrick road. We could have covered Gibbs Island and then stayed on the coast to Delamont. Anyway, this was probably one of the smallest islands I've circled, and it's also quite a safe island to get to, almost always accessible except maybe at a very high tide. I deliberately waited to visit this island until my son Daniel was home. We hadn't seen him since the previous Christmas. I think Brian appreciated Daniel (the 'second brother' as he calls him) joining us, holding his hand for most of the day.

Brian on Gibbs Island

We drove down from Bangor on a cold but sunny afternoon. Just south of Killyleagh we turned into Delamont Country Park and left our car there. We then took a circular route to the island, first going up to see the tall megalith stone. From the megalith, there is a lovely view across Strangford Lough and down to the Mournes. There's also a perfect view of the tree-covered Gibbs Island where we were heading. We then joined the coastal path, keeping the sea on our left and after a while, we climbed over a stone wall. This section is quite muddy, but Daniel, Brian and I were well prepared. There's a causeway across to the island, a small forest in the middle and a convenient grassy path around the island. We saw cows quietly grazing and all around us we could see a scattering of waterfowl making quite a lot of noise. I didn't recognise the various wildlife species, but apparently, at this time of the year the following ducks and birds can be seen; teal, wigeon, redshank, greenshank, jackdaws and rooks. I'm no expert, but there's one bird and sound I do recognise, and that's the lonely cry of the curlew! At the back of the island, it was a lot quieter. There's a small wooden bench which was the perfect place for our picnic, looking across at the other islands spread over Strangford.

Daniel and Brian enjoying our picnic on Gibbs Island

We could clearly see Gores Island, another tidal island where Brian and I walked around back in November 2019. We could even see the causeway to that island slowly fading away as the tide was coming in. On this side of Strangford Lough, we finished our picnic and left Gibbs Island as the winter sun was disappearing. So that's Stage 5 completed in full at last!

STAGE 6:

Co. Down: Comber to Portaferry

Sunday 23 July 2017

40 km or 24.9 miles

"Running doesn't build character, it reveals it."

We continued our adventure today in the village of Comber and keep following the 'coast' of Strangford Lough. This is our first run on a Sunday - all the others have been on a Saturday – and we're hoping the roads will be quieter this morning. We were glad too to get a short piece on Radio Ulster (Your Place and Mine) yesterday morning – good publicity for our cause!

Today I'm wearing my Clifton Hoka shoes which have been kindly donated by Pure Running. These are really amazing shoes – they literally give you a spring in your step, which is just as well because I need all the help I can get to try to keep up with Helen and Sean! Also, I think the name, Clifton Hokas shoes fit perfectly with our Clifton Run.

Our core team of three were delighted to be joined today at the start in Comber by Samantha Eakin, Debbie Matchett, Valerie McDonough, Claire Garrad, Rab Martin and Philip Mulligan.

I got to know young Samantha (Sam) recently – she works in StreetLife in Newtownards and always has a smile on her face. Debbie is my physio person and to be honest; I don't think I'd be doing this coastal run if it wasn't for her special treatment earlier in the year.

Valerie is a Tipperary girl, and of course, she is the excellent Chairperson of NDAC. Claire is a relative newcomer to running since returning to Bangor but is learning fast and building up her miles. Rab is a marathon runner and still turns out to play rugby for Donaghadee-not bad for a 49-year-old! And last but by no means least, is Philip - really the life and soul of any group.

The weather was dull enough to start with, and Scrabo Tower/Hill was covered in an early morning mist as we drove towards today's starting point. It was an earlier start today, and we leave Comber to start our run at about 7.40 am

Comber–the gateway to everywhere

Comber was once a very busy hub for three railway lines, Belfast to the west, Downpatrick and Newcastle to the south and Newtownards to the north – and today we're heading north towards Newtownards. I read somewhere that there was once a railway level crossing at Glassmoss (just outside Comber) that was 'operated by the Byers family for years' – no doubt ancestors of our own smooth operator, Helen Byers!

The mist is clearing, and as we're running along the Comber-Newtownards road, we have lovely views of Scrabo Hill and Scrabo Tower on our left-hand side. It's nice to note that Scrabo Tower (now just reopened) was built to honour Charles Stewart who was held in high regard with his attempts to alleviate suffering during the Irish Famine (one of the very few, kind and generous landlords of that time)

Floodgates Path

After about 2.5 miles outside Comber (halfway between Comber and N'Ards) we take a right turn through a farm-gate, leaving the dual carriageway and joining the Floodgates path. This is a beautiful stretch, completely traffic-free, although we are running close to the flight path at Newtownards Airport! We are lucky that we're running here in the early morning as we notice that today there is an Open Day at the Ards Airport. It's advertised as being 'perfect introduction to aviation for any budding pilots' -yes maybe best to get through this path as quick as possible!

We shortly emerge from the Floodgates path onto the Portaferry road just outside Newtownards. We continue south, and although we're on the main Newtownards-Portaferry road, we have a footpath to run on almost all the way as far as Greyabbey.

Rab, Sean, Philip and Debbie at Strangford Lough

Greyabbey

We learned that the Abbey here was the only Cistercian monastery in Ireland to be founded by a woman. Affreca established the Abbey here in 1193. A few centuries later in 1798, the United Irishmen, mainly inspired by Ulster Presbyterians were defeated here, and because of this, the men of the village were given the name *'the green boys of Greba'*. So it's only right we're wearing our (lime) green shirts as we run through Greyabbey!

Claire and Sam leave us at Greyabbey, and now there are seven of us left. Unfortunately, after this, we have no footpath for a little while, but we struggle along on the main road and eventually, we arrive in the quiet village of Kircubbin. (known as *'Cubinhillis'* in medieval times).

It's beautiful now on this side of the Ards Peninsula with lovely views across Strangford Lough to Whiterock and Daft Eddies (see also stage Five!), and we can still see Scrabo Tower in the distance. At this stage, Debbie, Valerie, Rab and Philip have to leave us.

So Helen, Sean and I proceed, and after about two or three miles south of Kircubbin we pass the Saltwater Brig Pub (I'm feeling thirsty all of a sudden!). On and on and then another mile or two of twisty roads south of Kircubbin we pass the townland of Ardkeen. Shortly after that we take a sharp right hand turn off the main road and enter Abbacy Road - glad to be on a much quieter road. Here we had arranged to meet Gerard Adair (a relative newcomer to NDAC). Gerard takes us to his friend Sharon Fitzsimons's house nearby (Sharon also happens to work with my wife, Maureen). Sharon had arranged a lovely spread of tea, cakes, biscuits and delicious banana bread. Maureen, our wee Brian and Sharon's daughter Ciara (recent All-Ireland Camogie Champion!) join us too. Also Sharon's friend, Monica Savage arrives and kindly donates to Clifton School.

After about half an hour, we reluctantly leave Sharon's house and continue along Abbacy Road with Gerard joining us for the last six miles into Portaferry.

Soon we see Castleward (on the other side of the Lough) in the distance. Even if we are tiring, it's still a beautiful run in along the shore to Portaferry, and we finally come to our finish line at the ferry port.

With Sean, Helen and Gerard in Portaferry, Co. Down

Stages 6 - Revisited: Island Hill, Comber, Co. Down

Sunday 10 November 2019

5.6 km or 3.5 miles

My son Brian and I decided to walk to this tidal island on a pleasant Sunday afternoon. We drove from Newtownards and just about 2 km before Comber we took a left turn, following the sign that said 'Islandhill' Car Park & Picnic area'. We parked in the car park and then walked across the causeway to Island Hill (also called Rough Island).

Brian crossing over onto Island Hill (or Rough Island) in Strangford

It didn't take us too long to circle this small island, and on the way back, along the causeway, we got chatting to a lady who pointed out some brent geese who had just arrived from Greenland – *'they're on their holidays'* the lady told us! Apparently 30,000 pale-bellied brent geese come here from Greenland every October to feed on the seagrass or eelgrass, which grows abundantly in Strangford Lough.

Tide coming in on Island Hill and soon this causeway will be covered

Also on Island Hill in 1936 a group of American archaeologists from Harvard carried out excavations and found evidence of occupation during the Mesolithic period (5,000 BC). So lots of people (and geese) have come and gone to this island over the years! Brian and I have now joined the club!

Stage 6 – Revisited: Strangford Islands, Co. Down (Chapel Island, Mid Island and South Island)

Sat. 30 May 2020

10.3 km or 6.4 miles

"The central place I call "Z" is in a valley surmounted by lofty mountains. The valley is about ten miles wide, and the city is on an eminence in the middle of it." (Percy Fawcett's letter to his son Brian, about his idea of the Lost City of 'Z'.)

Today was a walk (rather than run), and I was delighted to be joined by my two sons Matthew (who has just finished university) and Brian. Since the lockdown in March, the weather has been warm and sunny and today was no exception. We decided to tackle these three islands together, starting our walk from a small car park just south of Greyabbey on Strangford Lough.

Also, we thought it was wise to set out on our journey about 90 minutes before low tide. At the car park in Greyabbey, we could already see across the sands to a small cottage on Mid Island. There was no causeway from here, so we just headed in the direction of the white-washed cottage, getting our feet wet as we plodded through the sand and puddles until we reached Mid Island.

Mid Island

(Previously known as North Island and sometimes called Mid Isle). It was home to the Ulster-Scots poet Will McAvoy who lived in the cottage on the island - sometimes Will goes back to give poetry sessions. The island even became more famous recently as Brad Pitt's movie 'The Lost City of Z' was partly filmed here. This film was about the explorer Percy Fawcett who really became obsessed with finding the 'Lost City' in the Amazon Jungle. On his eighth and final expedition in 1925, he was joined by his 22-year-old son (same age as my son, Matthew!). Their last known communication was on 29 May 1925 (95 years ago yesterday), and the pair were never seen again. Fawcett's other younger son, Brian (yes, same name as my son) who remained in England, spent most of his life trying to find his father and brother.

I have great regard for all these great explorers. I have such admiration for the brave men who went to the South Pole like Amundsen, Scott, Shackleton and Crean. Now (after watching the film 'Lost City of Z') I am also so impressed with all that Percy Fawcett went through in South America and how it broadened his mind and built his character. Watching the movie, it was easy to spot Strangford Lough and Mid Island in certain scenes. Today I can almost imagine I'm an explorer in the Amazon Jungle – even the weather is slightly tropical!

My sons Matthew and Brian at Will McAvoy's cottage on Mid Island, Strangford Lough

South Island

I can now report that my two sons, Matthew and Brian, survived our own expedition to the three Strangford islands! Once we got to the cottage on Mid-Island, we took a left turn along the shore and walked along the track until we came to the causeway that took us over to South Island. Mid Island seems to have lots of vegetation/trees, but South Island is like one big open field, perfect for grazing (on a lovely sunny day like today) with its thick, lush grass, although we didn't see any cows or sheep.

Crossing causeway from Mid Island to South Island at Strangford Lough

When we arrived on South Island, we took a left turn immediately and then circled the whole island. We thought, when we got to the back (western side) of the island, we could then cut across to Chapel Island, but we realised that with soft mud and sand that it was much more practical (and quicker) to come back to the same causeway again that we took from Mid Island. We then walked around the other side of Mid Island (keeping the sea on our left) and eventually we could see Chapel Island in the distance.

There was no causeway from Mid Island to Chapel Island, so it was just a matter of ploughing through the sand, rocks, and water pools. I was glad Matthew was with me, and I think Brian enjoyed having Matthew (or as he calls him, the 'third brother') with him. We knew we were heading in the direction of the long island we presumed (correctly!) was Chapel Island. I was a bit concerned about the tide as it was now exactly low tide at 11.45 am. In hindsight, I need not have worried, and I think we would have been ok even two hours each side of low tide.

Chapel Island

As we got closer to Chapel Island, we veered to the left through the muddy rock pools so that we would arrive on the island on the southern side. We didn't expect to see an actual chapel on the island, but nevertheless, it is disappointing to see just a small broken wall of stones where I presume the church had once been!

All that remains of the chapel on Chapel Island, Strangford Lough

In any case, this was the perfect location to either pray or just sit and contemplate life in general. Of course, here right in the middle of Strangford Lough, we are very close to Nendrum (just over a mile across to the other side of the lough) where Saint Mahee had his monastery (on Mahee Island). No doubt the saint and his fellow monks were regular visitors to the chapel here. Matthew and Brian were happy too that we finally had our picnic with (360 degrees) views of the Mournes, Scrabo Tower and other islands on the lough.

Still we didn't delay too long as we were conscious that the 'tide was turning', and we still had to walk back the full length of the island (almost one mile long) before then taking to the wet sands again. Matthew suggested we walk towards the right (easterly directly) to return to our car quicker. Soon we were back on the mainland, and when we reached an old pier, we climbed up the embankment.

Heading home after circling the three islands on Strangford Lough!

Here we found a pleasant country trail along by the shore. That path soon faded away, but shortly we could see the cottage on Mid Island again, and we were back (where we started) at the car park in Greyabbey and enjoying another (well deserved!) picnic in the warm sunshine. Stage Six is now completed in full!

STAGE 7:

— ❖ —

Co. Down: Portaferry to Donaghadee

Saturday 12th August 2017

53 km or 32.9 miles

*"**Nana-korobi, ya-oki**" (fall down 7 times, get up 8 times). Old Japanese proverb*

We continued our challenge today, starting in the village of Portaferry and now running along the east side of the Ards Peninsula. I deliberately used that word 'challenge' (rather than adventure) because sometimes we forget how hard this task can be.

Our main team of three were delighted to be joined once again by Claire Garrad, Philip Mulligan and Sarah Benton, who is with us again for the third time. Today, we welcome Lindsay Doulton, a regular parkrunner, a Fulham supporter, and despite now being a young mother, still hasn't lost any of her fitness.

Starting team at Portaferry

It was an early start, leaving Portaferry at 7.45 am to make the most of the low tide and the lovely sandy beaches on this part of Co. Down. Today it seemed as if we were running all day long on mostly sandy surfaces and it gives me another excuse too to quote those lovely lines from De Profundis by Oscar Wilde

"the sea was for the swimmer, and the sand for the feet of the runner"

We had some sunshine and rain during the morning but not really a lot of either. Still, it was a perfect day for running, never reaching more than 17 degrees and with only a slight north wind blowing.

Anyway, we leave Portaferry and run south (yes South, as we're heading towards Bally-quintin Point at the very bottom of the Ards Peninsula). Remember, we're rigidly following the coast. It's a lovely quiet country road from Portaferry, and after about 3 miles we see a National Trust road/lane on the right leading back down towards the coast. In the distance, we see a cornfield, and when we reach the field, we notice a very narrow path which guides us nicely through the cornfield without causing any damage to the crop.

Running through the corn at very bottom of Ards Peninsula

We eventually leave the cornfield and come back onto a country road. After a few miles, we pass the entrance to St. Cooey's Wells.

St. Cooey died in 731, and these Wells have been a place of pilgrimage since then. A church here was pillaged by Norse pirates but was rebuilt again in the 12th century. Three different wells (washing, eye and drinking wells) are reputed to give special healing powers.

St. Cooey's Wells

St. Cooey's Wells

On Christmas Eve 2020, Brian and I visited the Wells. It was a beautiful sunny day and so clear that we could easily see the Isle of Man across the sea with the highest mountain on the island, Snaefell, very visible and clearly snow-capped! The only other person at St Cooey's Wells on that day was the local priest, Father Fergal McGrady (Brian was cheeky enough to ask him his name!) It was, of course, one of Fr. Fergal's predecessor's (Rev. David Morgan) who rediscovered and restored these ancient Wells back in the 1970s

Brian and Fr. Fergal at St. Cooey's Wells with Isle of Man behind

Meanwhile back in August 2017, the coastal runners drop down to the expansive Knock-inelder beach (I always smile when I hear Knockinelder - it sounds like pushing an old person over!). Shortly we pass a beautiful showpiece village called Kearney which has been restored by the National Trust. There is evidence of life here going back over a thousand years, and the old Slans Graveyard is nearby. The village of Kearney itself was used recently as a setting for a film 'My Mother and Other Strangers' set in WW2

Claire, Sarah and Helen on Cloughey strand

We are able to stay more or less on the beach, and soon we reach Cloughey. To travel by road by Portaferry to Cloughey is 5 miles but it took us (strictly coastal runners) 14.5 miles to get here. It's a beautiful long beach at Cloughey and with the low tide, perfect for the feet of us runners.

Gerry and Claire silhouetted at Cloughey Beach

Farewell to Lindsay and Claire at Cloughey

We are sad to say goodbye to Lindsay and Claire, and now there are five of us left. We continue through the sand dunes and bushes at Cloughey. Even though it's still early August, we notice the blackberries are already ripe.

At Portavogie they're getting ready for a Seafood Festival here, but unfortunately, we haven't time to wait. Also at Portavogie, we should note that for a time Georgie Best and his wife Alex moved here for a much quieter life.

Just north of Portavogie we pass Burr Point, the most easterly point on the island of Ireland. Looking out to sea in the distance we can see the Isle of Man towards our right and Scotland on our left. Sean also points out the Scafell Mountain Range straight across in Cumbria (Lake District) which we can just about make out, well Sean thinks he can see it!

Remembering Lisa

Next we come to the village of Ballyhalbert, and as we run along the beautiful strand opposite the many caravan sites, we are reminded of a tragic day over twelve years ago. The day was 28 February 2005 when a young lady called Lisa Dorrian went missing. It's believed she was murdered here at Ballyhalbert, but her body has yet to be found.

After Ballyhalbert, the shore is rough and rocky, and reluctantly we have to move up onto the main A2 for a few miles. However, we're soon down on the shore again, and now we can see the church steeple of Ballywalter in the distance. It's another long (very long!) sandy beach all the way into the village. I can feel my legs getting heavy now - this sand is hard work for the runner's feet (and legs)! I think we were all glad to have a wee break at Ballywalter (formerly known as Whitkirk).

I think it was about a mile before Millisle when it happened! I hit the wall and felt like a car that had just run out of petrol! I struggled on for a while and managed to get as far as Millisle village. I insisted that we stop in Millisle (for coffee and chocolate) even though we were only about two miles from Donaghadee, our final destination. I eventually regained my energy and recovered. Soon we were running again, and shortly we reached *'the Commons'*, a lovely green area outside Donaghadee.

Then we spotted it in the distance – and yes there it was - and never was I so glad to see it -that iconic Lighthouse in Donaghadee. We even had a welcoming crowd to spur us along as we ran down to the Lighthouse at the end of the pier.

Sarah and the welcoming party at Donaghadee Lighthouse

Melanie Patton (another friend from NDAC), Claire (who ran with us earlier) and their lovely children were all there clapping and cheering us along the pier. Melanie even produced orange juice and delicious donuts (or gravy rings as they're called in Northern Ireland!). Just what we needed after 33 miles!

And once again Helen rounded off another great day with a swim in the sea ......and so our adventure continues.

Helen cooling down in Donaghadee after running 53 km

STAGE 8:

❖

Co. Down: Donaghadee to Belfast

Saturday 16 September 2017

40 km or 24.9 miles

"Only those who will risk going too far can possibly find out how far they can go". TS Elliot

This was our final Co. Down stage in very familiar territory. Sean is from Donaghadee and both Helen and I live in Bangor, so the three of us knew exactly where we were going today. We hadn't to worry about the tide either as we had a proper coastal path almost all of the way to Belfast. We were running from east to west today with a nice view across to the south Antrim coast and Scotland (Dumfries and Galloway) clearly visible in the distance

Our main team of three met at 7.15 am at Donaghadee Lighthouse (where we finished on 12 Aug) and we were delighted to be joined once again by Sarah, Claire and Jill. Also we welcomed five new first-timers today, Melanie Patton, Donald Smith, Johnny Mc-Grath, Michael Roberts and Lynne Kerr.

Melanie has been such a good supporter of ours, ever since we came up with this crazy idea last October. Donald is another ultra-marathon runner, having recently completed 100 miles in a 24-hour challenge! Johnny is founder of the Sunday Morning Running/ Coffee group - not sure if Johnny or I will make it tomorrow morning! Michael is a dedicated coach with NDAC and has worked with and encouraged runners of all ages over the years. Lynne is another impressive NDAC Coach and trains various groups of runners on Monday and Wednesday nights. So that's eleven runners today, and ten of us started in Donaghadee. Lynne joined us later in Bangor.

Donaghadee

Two very famous songwriters/poets both referred to Donaghadee in their songs, although neither has actually been here! Johnny Cash mentions Donaghadee in his 'Forty Shades of Green' and Thomas Hardy wrote as follows:

> *"I've never gone to Donaghadee, That vague far townlet by the sea; In Donaghadee I shall never be: Then why do I sing of Donaghadee"*

Another famous writer Brendan Behan painted the Lighthouse, and I don't mean drawing a picture of it! He was responsible for maintaining it and by all accounts failed miserably at his task! Remember we passed St. John's Lighthouse in May (Stage 4) which Behan also tried to maintain.

Once again, we were mostly lucky with the weather. It seems like it's been raining every day since July, but we had a bright sky for most of the day. We run along the main coastal road towards Bangor but after about 2.5 miles (at the car park and opposite the Portavoe Reservoir) we go through a gate/gap in the fence and find a narrow coastal path. Shortly afterwards we climb steep steps, and now we are running on the edge of a low cliff with the Copeland Islands so close on our right-hand side. We are really in the townland of Orlock now. We follow this path on the edge of the sea, descend some steps and then shortly go through a narrow tunnel cut through the rocks. We're running along a wide path here known as 'the old coach road'. There is evidence here of a more significant path, wide enough for a carriage. Nobody is sure what this wider path was used for, but the consensus is that it was probably used for smuggling. Other evidence suggests that there were bridges across some sea inlets similar to the Gobbins in Islandmagee (see Stage 9) and this might have been part of another 'adrenaline adventure'!

Jill leading the way on the coastal path from Groomsport

We eventually arrive in the small harbour village of Groomsport -home to the famous Eagle Wing Ship that didn't quite make it to America. The boat set sail in 1636 and had already completed three-quarters of America's journey (in the strong winds and storms) when Captain/Reverend Blair decided to turn back. Reverend Blair saw the extreme weather as a sign of God telling him (and all on board) to return to Ireland. The Boat is still remembered in Groomsport's annual Eagle Wing festival.

We continue along the coastal path from Groomsport. Sean takes us right around the white house on the west side of Groomsport. Soon we arrive on the long Ballyholme Beach (so familiar to us all and my home is only a mile from here). We leave Ballyholme beach and follow the coast along a quiet road (Seacliff Road) running on the footpath into Bangor town centre.

Shortly we pass by Eisenhower Pier and are reminded of Bangor's connection to WW2. Eisenhower visited here to review the troops and ships gathered in Bangor Bay prior to launching D-Day landings in 1944.

So, the ten of us arrive at Ward Park in Bangor at about 9.15 just in time to run the Bangor parkrun.

Bangor parkrun

There are now 86 different parkruns on the island of Ireland, and the numbers are growing all the time! Bangor parkrun, with an average of 259 runners every week (one week there was 420) is the most popular parkrun in N.Ireland and excluding Dublin, Bangor is the most popular parkrun in all of Ireland.

We pop into run Bangor parkrun during North Down section

We get a great welcome from everyone at the parkrun and we've already completed 13 miles this morning. After we finish the parkrun we are treated to a great spread of tea, buns, biscuits and cakes by Alison, Debbie, Brenda and their team.

The Cannon in Ward Park was the main gun on the German U-19 U-boat during WW1. After the surrender of the U-boat in 1918, the Cannon was donated to Bangor in recognition of Commander Bingham VC (who was born in Bangor – we share the same birthday). Interestingly the German Captain of the U-boat, Weisbach had previously served as torpedo officer on the U-boat that sank the Lusitania in 1915 (which was really the deciding factor in America entering WW1) Also, during his brief command of the U-19, Herr Weisbach delivered Sir Roger Casement from the U19 U-boat to Banna Strand in Co. Kerry in April 1916. The knighted Casement, who had switched allegiance to the Irish cause, was captured shortly after arriving on the Kerry beach and hanged for treason in June 1916. (I refer to Casement again in Stage 12.)

Ward Park Cannon of U19 U Boat in Bangor, Co. Down

Only Claire continues with the regular three and we welcome Lynne as we continue on towards Belfast.

At the McKee Clock in Bangor, we also meet up with some other Clifton School parents (Janis & friends, and the Nickell family too). We had arranged our run to coincide with the annual Clifton walk from Bangor to Holywood. Maureen and our son Brian also walk with us for a short while.

At the Pickie Park in Bangor, we leave the walkers, and the five of us continue running along the coastal path. We really enjoyed today, passing all those familiar and beautiful places that we've walked and run so many times, Strickland's Glen, Crawfordsburn and Helen's Bay (named after Helen Blackwood aka Lady Dufferin)

On the Pickie Puffer in Bangor with special boys, Conor and Brian

Running along the N. Down coastal path, we pass by a lot of golf courses here. Of course, our own local hero, Rory McIlroy (from nearby Holywood) learned his trade. We get a nice surprise at Cultra when Michael Stitt, our colleague from NDAC comes to meet us and cheer us on.

Claire, Lynne, Sean, Gerry and Helen at the new footbridge at Seahill

We arrive in Holywood at about 12.15, and sadly Claire and Lynne leave us here. We stay by the coast at the Dirty Duck pub, following a narrow, traffic-free road and eventually we arrive at a big office building (Clare House) on the outskirts of Belfast at Airport Road West. We're obviously very near George Best City Airport now and are very much aware of low flying aircraft coming in to land.

We continue along Airport Road West towards Belfast. Is this the longest road in N.Ireland or did it just feel like that? We're tiring now too, the bright sky has disappeared, and the rain is coming down. Helen and Sean give me some encouragement by announcing that we've now done exactly 200 miles of our run! We can now see the famous Harland & Wolff yellow cranes towering in the distance (known locally as Samson and Goliath). These mark the spot where the great Titanic was built in 1912 although the cranes weren't erected until the early seventies.

At the iconic 'Harland and Wolff Cranes' in Belfast

Of course the Co.Down border is geographically the River Lagan and soon we arrive by the river at the fabulous new Titanic Building. The rain is coming down now, it's turned out to be miserable day, but Helen, Sean and I are so delighted and relieved to have finally got to Belfast and completed the whole Co. Down coast.

At the Titanic Building in Belfast

As an extra bonus, Helen has arranged with her friend Ruth Cleland (who worked at Titanic) to take us up to the very top of the Titanic Building where we get amazing views of the river Lagan and Belfast. This was definitely the perfect place to finish the Co. Down stage of our coastal challenge.

Stage 8 - Revisited: Friend Island, Groomsport, Co. Down.

Saturday 9 May 2020

No extra mileage

I'm probably going too far in calling this an island as it's so small and so close to the shore. However it passes the test as an island - surrounded by water for most of the time! It lies just west of Groomsport, and I was always aware it was there as I often ran along that coastal path from Ballyholme beach. I used to call it the 'sandy island' as it has a lovely silver beach that shines as it catches the sun, but then I saw a wooden sign on the Groomsport side saying 'Friend Island'.

Brian with Friend Island behind

If you're running (or walking) from Ballyholme to Groomsport along the coastal path, the nicest way to approach it (at low tide of course!) it is to take a left turn by the coast at about the half way point. Follow this rougher outer coastal path, and it will eventually take you across some stepping stones to Friend Island. During the first lockdown (March to June 2020) the weather was lovely and dry, and I often ran (or walked with Brian) to the island. Then on 9th May 2020, Maureen and I decided to get up at 4.00 am and watch the sunrise. This was in support of the 'Darkness into Light' campaign (which helps raise awareness of suicide and self-harm). At the crack of dawn, Maureen and I walked down to Ballyholme beach and then along an outer coastal path towards Groomsport. At first, as it was slightly cloudy, we couldn't see any sunrise. However, just as we arrived on the island, we could see the sun slowly rising over Groomsport. It was definitely worth getting up to see!

STAGE 9:

❖

Co. Antrim: Belfast to Islandmagee

Saturday 7 October 2017

39.9 km or 24.8 miles

"Keep your eyes on the stars, and your feet on the ground". Theodore Roosevelt

We started our run today in the city of Belfast which borders two counties, Co. Down on the east of the river Lagan and Co. Antrim on the west side. We've already completed all 200 miles of the Co. Down coast (from February to September) and this morning we crossed the river to complete the rest of N.Ireland.

At the SS Nomadic – this boat was used to ferry people from shore to Titanic

Helen, Sean and I were delighted to be joined in Belfast by Claire Garrad (Claire's fourth run with us). So, the four of us start together at 8.45am at the new Titanic building. It's quite busy in the Titanic Quarter even at this time of the morning and great to see this whole area being revitalised. Once we cross the river, we take a right turn, passing the 'Big Fish' or 'Salmon of Knowledge', remembering the story of how Fionn McCumhaill got his wisdom. We're heading north now, and we go under the M3 Motorway and come to Donegal Quay.

Sean gains some 'salmon knowledge' at River Lagan, Belfast

Sailortown

We pass through the old docks area of Belfast, known locally as Sailor Town. A local guy, Anthony Tonor wrote a great song in 2010 about this neighbourhood. He called it Sailortown and started singing it in the nearby Rotterdam Bar.

'The walls in the city have a lot to say, about the UVF and the IRA but these walls say nothing about who I am, when I'm singing in the garden at the Rotterdam, doing Brown Eyed Girl and Whiskey In The Jar."

At this stage Helen and Sean head across to north Belfast to the Waterworks parkrun. Claire and I continue through Sailortown. My hip has been giving me problems again, and I'm lucky to have Claire to run with. The four of us arrange to meet later in Carrickfergus.

Claire and I continue along Corporation Street, and eventually, we join the Cycle/Walk path with the M2/M5 Motorway close by on our left. This is actually part of the route of the Belfast Marathon. We pass Hazelbank Park, and even when we get to Gideons Green, we still have a promenade and wide footpath to run on. The sky is very grey now, and we struggle through the showers without getting too wet. We pass Jordonstown, Greenisland and arrive in Carrickfergus. Claire measures it as 11 miles so far, and we can relax here in Carrick, knowing we still have to wait for Helen and Sean to arrive.

For a period in the 17th century, Carrick was larger and more prominent than Belfast and back then Belfast Lough was known as Carrickfergus Bay. William of Orange arrived here in 1690 on his way to the Battle of the Boyne where he defeated his father-in-law, King James.

Claire and I had arranged to meet Helen and Sean in Creeds Cafe in Carrick, and we manage to get into the cafe before the heavy rain. We get nice seats on high stools by the window, drinking our tea and coffee. Eventually we spot the two lime green shirts (and Helen's new pink shoes!) in the distance.

We leave Carrick, and we're still able to run by the shore on a wide footpath. About a mile after leaving Carrick we take a right turn at Magills Avenue and arrive at what once was a separate village (and strangely named!) Boneybefore. Apparently in 1760 French soldiers were told that this village was *"a bonny wee place just before Carrick"*. The house where US President Andrew Jackson's parents lived is also here.

President Jackson

Andrew Jackson served as the seventh US president from 1829 to 1837 and was involved in what is believed to be the first attempt to kill a sitting President when someone aimed a pistol at Jackson, which misfired. Luckily for the president, the brave Davy Crockett happened to be there (the right man in the right place!) and restrained and disarmed the culprit.

At 'Boneybefore' near Carrickfergus where President Jackson's parents lived

We continue here close to the railway line (and away from the main road), and then along by 'Old Turn' road, leading to Loughview Drive which turns into a rough (and flooded) path. We arrive back out on the main Whitehead road at the village of Eden. Nobody said this adventure would lead us to Paradise, but today we did reach a place called the 'Garden of Eden'. We couldn't resist a good photo opportunity here, and Helen even popped into a local shop to buy some apples!

Apples in the Garden of Eden!

It's a busy road as we leave Eden, but at least we have a footpath (sometimes very narrow!) all the way to Whitehead. As we come into Whitehead, we take a right turn into Prince of Wales Avenue and arrive at the railway station. Whitehead is the town with no streets - it has no streets with the suffix *'street'* in its name - so no High Street or Main Street. We stick to the coast, passing by lovely buildings in contrasting colours and follow the Blackhead Path to the Lighthouse. It's a tough climb up to the Lighthouse (lots of steps!) but well worth it for the magnificence views across the Lough and over to Scotland. Better still, the weather is improving now, the sun is even threatening to shine, and the blackberries are still available for us hungry runners!

Sean, Claire and Gerry at Blackhead Lighthouse

We leave the Lighthouse and run downhill along a narrow (almost traffic-free) road called McCraes Brae. We soon join up with the 'main' Ballystrudder road and take a right, heading north into the heart of Islandmagee. Somehow the conversation turns to ice-cream, and Claire and Helen have heard rumours that the 'The Rinkha' in Islandmagee do the best ice-cream in N.Ireland. Of course, we stop for ice-cream at the Rinkha, which lives up to its reputation! We cross the road here in Ballystrudder and take a right turn into Gobbins Road. Unfortunately for us, the famous Gobbins cliff path walk is closed today. However, a few years later (see below), I go back and complete this fantastic cliff walk with my wife Maureen and son Brian.

Today in October 2017 it's turning out to be a lovely day. The sun has come out now, the sky and sea are blue, and when we reach the top, there are lovely views of the Gobbins cliff path just below us. It's a long hill and challenging climb up the Gobbins Road (and my legs are letting me down again!) After about another 3 miles along Gobbins Road, we eventually come to a T junction. We take a right turn into Middle Road and finally reach our destination at Earls Cafe, Mulloughboy. The proprietor at Earls is Shalana, who has a friendly welcome for us and we are glad to tuck into some excellent homemade food. (Shalana also donates to Clifton School). We tell her we'll back in 5 weeks for the start of Stage 10 of our coastal run.

October 2017: Claire, Sean and Helen on Gobbins Road

Stage 9 – Revisited: Gobbins Cliff path walk, Islandmagee, Co. Antrim

Sunday 13 December 2020

No extra mileage

This cliff path was closed when Helen, Claire, Sean and I were here in October 2017 so it was nice to include this famous section. I love the original description of these types of walks where they call it an 'adrenaline adventure'. It sums up my experience when I went back with Maureen and Brian to complete this section of the coastal path! The Gobbins is a cliff-path on the east side of Islandmagee. It runs across bridges, past caves and through a tunnel. The Gobbins was created for the Belfast Railway Company and first opened to the public in 1902. Advertisements of the time declared '*the new cliff path with its ravines, bore caves, natural aquariums ... has no parallel in Europe as a marine cliff walk*' ...but when the railway company got into financial difficulties the path was closed in the 1930s. However, from 2011-2015, Larne Borough Council led a project to reopen The Gobbins. A series of new bridges and galleries were constructed and installed during 2014-15.

I was surprised that we were allowed go on the walk today as it was so wet and windy. To make the conditions worse, it was also high tide but more about that later!

Maureen and Brian at the start of Gobbins walk

We had the usual safety instructions at the Gobbins Centre, but nothing prepared us for the actual walk itself. Our guide said it was the worst conditions he'd seen in two years. There were eight in our group, but only three made it to the tubular bridge at the end of the cliff walk!

Brian and Maureen at the Gobbins

It's a fascinating walk. The rope barriers protect you, but, when those waves come crashing, they shock you and wet you to the core!

Crashing waves at high tide!

We were unlucky with strong winds, rain and a high tide that caught us at the perfect time. A couple (in our group) with a ten-year-old girl turned back halfway into the walk. We were all soaked to the skin at that stage, and Maureen and Brian had had enough too.

I carried on walking with a young couple, but soon another massive wave washed that young lady literally off her feet. She was still brave enough to keep going. The three of us got wetter and wetter as the waves kept crashing against the rocks until we finally crossed over the original tubular bridge. Yes, that was an adrenaline adventure and a nice way to complete Stage 9.

STAGE 10:

❖

Co. Antrim: Islandmagee to Larne

Saturday 11 November 2017

43 km or 26.7 miles

'If you can take it, you can make it' *Louie Zamperini*

Dawn is just breaking as we arrive on the peninsula of Islandmagee to start stage 10 of our coastal adventure. Since our run last month we've had Hurricane Ophelia and Storm Brian, but today the weather wasn't too bad at all – a little cool, but we quickly warm up after a mile or two.

Islandmagee-the Beanies

In early medieval times, Islandmagee was known as *'Semne'*, and we met a lady who told us that the native Islandmagee people are known as *'beanies'*. This comes from the fact that beans were grown here to supply nitrogen to the soil years ago.

It's just the three regular runners today and it's the first coastal run on our own since April (Kilkeel to Dundrum).

We leave Earls Cafe and continue north along Mulloughboy Road leading us down to the lovely Browns Bay beach. We continue along the shore passing by Larne Golf course on our right and then taking a left into Ballylumford road. We're now running along the west side of the Peninsula, and shortly we pass the site of Northern Ireland's main power station at Ballylumford.

96

I had read somewhere that there was a ferry crossing between Ballylumford and Larne. I rang the ferry company, and they informed me that due to insufficient demand, the ferry stopped running 18 months ago. Anyway, as Helen says *'we don't do shortcuts or ferries'*.

About a mile further south, we pass the 'Druids Altar' Dolmen. This monument dates to 2500BC and some archaeologists even date it as a Neolithic Tomb dating back as far as 4000 BC. We can even go back further than that (like 200 million years ago!) to discover that dinosaurs were once present in this area. Islandmagee is the only place in Ireland where traces of dinosaurs were ever found (bones from a four-legged scelidosaurus and bones from a two-legged carnivore sarcosaurus were discovered recently)

The' Druids Altar' Dolmen on Islandmagee

As we continue running, we realise that Islandmagee is quite hilly and in fact, hills dominate our whole story today! It might be a coastal run, but this morning we seemed to be climbing all the time.

Witchcraft Trial

In 1710 eight women in Islandmagee were convicted of witchcraft and sentenced to a year's imprisonment. As recently as 2015 a memorial was proposed by the author Martina Devlin. However the memorial was objected to by a TUV (Traditional Unionist Voice) councillor who believed the plaque could become a "shrine to paganism" and furthermore Mr. McKee stated that he wasn't convinced that the women weren't guilty!

We continue along Ballylumford Road which joins up with Millbay Road on the west side of Islandmagee, keeping the sea (as always!) on our right-hand side. We come back onto the Low Road, take a right turn at a wee roundabout, and sadly leave Islandmagee.

I should mention that Helen was worried that today's stage would be too short, so to appease her, I planned a slight diversion inland to add a few more miles to our journey! We cross the bridge (leaving the Islandmagee peninsula) and decide not to take the main/ busy road into Larne. Instead we cross the road and head up to the village of Ballycarry. It's a tough (and long!) climb up to Ballycarry, but the views from the top are worth it as we look back across to Islandmagee and Scotland in the distance. We take a right turn at the top of the hill into Hillhead Road.

Ballycarry

Ballycarry, previously called Broadisland, boasts the oldest Presbyterian congregation in Ireland - founded in 1613. It's also the home of James Orr (known as the Bard of Bally-carry) who wrote 'the Irishman' which contains the famous lines

'The savage loves his native shore, though rude the soil and chill the air.'

We continue along the quiet country roads through Hillhead Road which joins up with Ballypollard Road, and eventually we come to the beautiful village of Glenoe. We face another tough climb (more hills!) up to Glenoe Waterfall.

Helen's face says it all!

I don't think Helen is really that impressed with my 'inland diversion' and admittedly the terrain here is not as flat as the coastal route! However Sean is not complaining and is now in complete ultra-marathon mode as he sprints up the steep hill in Glenoe. We're now four miles inland so maybe it is time to head back to the coast again.

At its Remembrance Day today (11 November), we pause to pay our respects at the War Memorial at the village of Glynn. We're now only two miles from the town of Larne.

Friends' Goodwill

Exactly 300 years ago in 1717 a small ship called 'Friends Goodwill' made her way out of Larne Harbour as one of the first emigrant boats to cross the Atlantic. The vessel encountered a storm, food ran low, and it was reported that the crew caught sharks and dolphins for food and collected rain water on the deck. The voyage's historical account tells us that things were so bad that lots were drawn as to who would be eaten first when the worst extremity came. Thankfully in September 1717 (four months after leaving Larne), the City Commissioners in Boston were apparently informed that 'Forty-nine miserable persons arrived from ye North of Ireland on a single vessel.'

Sean has a 'romantic connection' with Larne (his wife Patricia!) and so can guide us through the town and eventually down to the coast at the majestic Chaine Round Tower (built in 1888 as a memorial to James Chaine, an MP who developed Larne as a sea port). As it happens, Larne Athletic Club is just finishing their Club Handicap Race today beside the tower. We stop to chat with some local runners outside the Leisure Centre, and they offer us tea, coffee and biscuits - just what we needed before we complete the last three miles to Drains Bay!

At Chaine Tower in Larne

It's a lovely run in along the Antrim Coast, passing under the famous Black Cave Tunnel and finally arriving in Carnfunnock Park at 1.00 pm.

At Black Cave Tunnel outside Larne

STAGE 11:

❖

Co. Antrim: Larne to Cushendall

Saturday 16 December 2017

35.9 km or 22.3 miles

'Winter Miles makes Summer Smiles' Dennis Scott (NDAC)

With only nine days to Christmas Day, today's run had a kind of festive feeling about it. The green glens of Antrim were still covered in snow to add to the occasion. And to complete the whole picture, Helen was wearing her Christmas hat with ringing bells!

We have to thank Laura McAllister (Helen's friend) for meeting us in Cushendall and driving us back to our start at Drains Bay (just north of Larne) – that saved us having to take two cars today!

We were delighted too that Laura's husband, Phelim ran with us for most of the way today. Phelim, Laura and their son Jude live in the beautiful village of Glenarm and Phelim took time off from plucking turkeys to join us on the Antrim coast. However with both Phelim and Sean supporting similar beards, shorts and shirts, it was very confusing at times today!

Sean came straight from the night-shift for today's run. He also had a wee 100 mile run last week through the Wicklow Mountains, so maybe he'll go easy on us today. Meanwhile Debbie from PhysioWorks is keeping my body in order and has given me special exercises which involve moving my pelvis without moving any other part of my body - easy enough to do (if you happen to be a Hawaiian dancer!)

It was 9.00 am (just after sunrise) when we got to Drains Bay (just north of Larne), and in our wisdom, we decided to tackle the Larne parkrun that takes place in Drains Bay. We received a great welcome from the organisers of the Larne parkrun, and we even got the benefit of a local photographer (Bill Guiller) who also caught up with us later at Glenarm and took more pictures there. Thank you Bill!

After completing the parkrun we eventually leave Drains Bay at 10.30 am. Such a beautiful part of the world today in Co. Antrim and we had the perfect weather with blue skies and lovely sunshine as we reached the village of Glenarm. Glenarm is the first of Antrim's nine glens and claims to be the oldest town in Ulster having been granted a charter in the 12th century.

We hugged the coast the whole day, passing through such lovely villages and enjoying amazing views across to Scotland, with the Mull of Kintyre now only about 20 miles away. Also the tall and rocky island of Ailsa Craig could be clearly seen in the distance jutting up from the Irish Sea. (The Ailsa Craig Island/Rock is still for sale and reduced now to £1.5m, down from original £2.5m – a bargain I'd say!)

At Glenarm on Antrim coast

We leave Glenarm, and the sun is still shining as we arrive in Carnlough, which is probably our half way point today. Churchill's great grandmother built the Londonderry Arms in Carnlough and years later when Churchill visited he met the postmistress "I've come to see the village founded by my great-grandmother", he said. "Mr. Churchill", she replied "Carnlough existed long before her."

A beautiful rainbow appears over the hills which really should have warned us that rain was ahead! Sean stops to take pictures of the rainbow, but Helen, Phelim and I carry on towards Waterfoot along the winding Antrim Coastal Road.

On Antrim Coast Road

Antrim Coast Road

The 40 km coast road (Larne to Cushendall) that we're running along today was built by William Bald between 1832 and 1842. Bald also had the unique idea to blast the cliff face which then fell onto the foreshore to form the new road base. Up to that point, there were no proper roads in this area, and the 13 miles of sea to Scotland was the easiest trading route.

Phelim has to leave us (more turkeys to pluck!) and so Helen and I carry on to Waterfoot with Sean (still trying to stay awake) a few hundred metres behind. Gradually the sun disappears, replaced by the rain and wind and the temperature drops. It's a real struggle now to keep going in such miserable conditions.

Helen, Gerry and Phelim (another bearded runner)

My body and especially my feet are suffering (and blistering!). I was listening to Radio Ulster last month about a traveller/explorer from Castlerock called Leon McCarron. He described how he was walking through Jordan after a long day's trekking when a local man invited him into his home and proceeded to wash Leon's feet. If only we could be so lucky today on the Antrim coast!

Helen and I eventually reach the outskirts of Waterfoot and very slowly make our way (walking/running) to the village's centre. We stop at a shop for drinks, and the girl there tells us (the greatest news!) 'it's only one more mile to Cushendall'. We wait outside the shop for Sean, and when he arrives, we continue together for the final stretch. It might be one of the shortest days in the year, but it seemed a long, long time since I parked my car in Cushendall this morning. And so Christmas is almost here ...and our adventure continues again next year in 2018.

STAGE 12:

❖

Co. Antrim: Cushendall to Ballycastle (via Tor Head)

Saturday 20 January 2018

31 km or 19.3 miles

"Nothing hurts more, but is so rewarding at the same time" Sandy Zanchi

It seems a long time ago since our previous monthly coastal run which was just before Christmas. Today was all about the snow and ice! Running through the snow in the sunshine was at times invigorating, and we were able to push along on a perfect soft surface. However, the ice was another story – sometimes it was quite dangerous, and we had to tip-toe our way through the treacherous spots of black ice. As usual, we started where we finished, and so we continued our adventure today in 2018 in the village of Cushendall, Co. Antrim.

It was way back in a primary school in Galway when I first heard the magical (and scary!) name of Cushendall as part of a short poem I learned.

"Tiveragh is a fairy hill and near to Cushendall, and nobody goes there at night, no nobody at all" John Irvine Desmond

Cushendall (formerly known as Newtown Glens) is the meeting point of three of Antrim's famous Glens. To add to the mystery and folklore, Cushendall is also supposed to be the burial place of Oisin who ran off with Niamh to Tír na nÓg (land of the young) but then Oisin foolishly returned to Ireland and turned into an old man. He didn't realise that he had spent hundreds of years in Tír na nÓg where nobody ever grew old! Helen, Sean and I were delighted to be joined by Helena Dornan, an experienced ultra runner (and friend of Sean's) from North Antrim. Helena even met us in Ballycastle (our finish point) and drove us through the snow and ice back to Cushendall where we began today's run. Thank you Helena! We started today in Cushendall with snow-covered Lurig Mountain towering over the village. We continue along Shore Road which leads on to Layde Road to the ruins of Layde Church, dating back to 1638 and one of the main burial places of the MacDonnells. We follow the icy coast road to Cushendun, and we struggle through the slippery surface. At times it was like running on Dundonald Ice Bowl!

With Helena on icy Cushendall to Cushendun road

We arrive eventually in Cushendun, which is the nearest Irish village to Scotland. In fact, before the Act of Union in 1800, Cushendun had its own Customs House and Passport Office, and this would have been the main entry point from Scotland.

In Cushendun at the statue of Johann (the last animal to be culled during 2001 foot and mouth epidemic)

We leave Cushendun and continue to hug the coast and climb the narrow road towards Torr Head. The views are spectacular today in the winter sunshine and snow. However, once again, the icy surface slows us down. It seems like hours have passed before we eventually reach Torr Head, and when we get there, we climb up the steep hill to the ruins of Altagore Castle. From Torr Head there are fabulous views east towards the Mull of Kintyre (and the island of Arran) and north towards Rathlin and the island of Islay. We've finally arrived at the north easterly corner of Ireland.

Standing at Torr Head, we're only 13 miles from the Mull of Kintyre in Scotland. Last week, I talked to Billy Brannigan, a North Down AC veteran, who now lives in Campbeltown on the Mull of Kintyre. Billy explained how Paul McCartney, not only made the place famous by the song 'Mull of Kintyre' but he also wrote the classic 'The Long and Winding Road' on his farm near Campbeltown. McCartney was inspired by the sight of a road *"stretching up into the hills in the calm beauty in the remote highlands surroundings"*.

Torr Head: Helen, Helena and Sean on Torr Head, Co. Antrim

Of course this side of the Irish Sea has its own calm beauty as we leave Torr Head and continue west along our own long and winding road. It seems safer now. Earlier, all four of us had fallen over at some stage along the slippery surfaces. Thankfully none of us was injured, and we're still going strong. We have this narrow road all to ourselves today and a beautiful white surface to run on. It even seems warm now in the winter sunshine as we power through the soft snow. We soon come to the junction at Murlough Bay and the four of us stop to discuss whether we should tackle the slippery cliff tops of Fair Head or continue along the narrow road.

We agree for safety reasons not to go to Murlough Bay, and so we avoid the 'Grey Mans Path' along Fair Hill. Helena, our local guide today keeps us safe, and as we get close to Ballycastle (her home town) we take a right turn down Drumaroan Road which leads us towards the beach. It's the perfect way to approach the beautiful town of Ballycastle with Rathlin Island stretching across in the near distance.

As we continue our adventure, we are thinking about other people who also travelled this route. Terry Eakin, of course, completed the whole coast of Northern Ireland in 2013 and referred to a man called David Boyd who apparently walked around the whole coast of Ireland in the 1980's. Terry tells us that David's ashes are scattered somewhere around Torr Head. Also I've just heard last week about a lady called Mary Nolan Hickey who started her own epic adventure, running around Ireland. Mary has run every Dublin Marathon since it started in 1980 and she's now running every day to try to 'lap the map' of Ireland. She's doing it to raise funds for RNLI. I met her on 17 January and ran with her from Donaghadee to Belfast.

Stage 12: Co. Antrim: Revisited: Fair Head to Ballycastle:

Sat. 13 June 2020

10.3 km or 6.4 miles

"Take my body back with you and let it lie in the old churchyard in Murlough Bay" (Roger Casements last wish before he was executed)

Back in January 2018 with icy roads and cliffs, we took the decision not to tackle the coast around Fair Head. However I always intended to complete this section and so in June 2020 I went back. It turned out to be a beautiful day. We left Bangor, Co. Down at about 10.30 am and drove to north Antrim. Maureen, our sons (Matthew and Brian) and I decided to stop off in Armoy (about 10 km south of Ballycastle) at the 'Dark Hedges' made famous by the drama 'Game of Thrones'. It was our first time here, and we were privileged to be the only visitors today at the hanging trees.

Leaving the 'Dark Hedges' made famous in 'Game of Thrones'

Afterwards, we drove on to nearby Ballycastle and then to that exact spot on the road from Torr Head where it's signposted to Murlough Bay. (not to be confused with Murlough in Co. Down). This was the route we decided to avoid in January 2018 because of the ice and snow. So, Maureen and the boys let me off at that junction to continue Stage 12 on my own again.

From there I ran down the steep, narrow winding road to Murlough Bay, passing a big Cross as the lovely blue Sea of Moyle opened up in front of me. The Cross and nearby plaque were dedicated to Roger Casement.

Sir Roger Casement

There is a lot of discussion now about pulling down statues of slave traders, but Casement actually fought against human rights abuses in the Congo and Peru and campaigned for the anti-slavery society. He was knighted in 1911 for his work against these atrocities. Later he became an anti-imperialist and joined the Irish Rebels. During the 1916 rebellion, he tried to import arms from Germany and was dropped off in a U boat (U19) in

Co. Kerry where he was captured and then hanged for high treason. Diaries indicating his homosexually were also used against him in his trial.

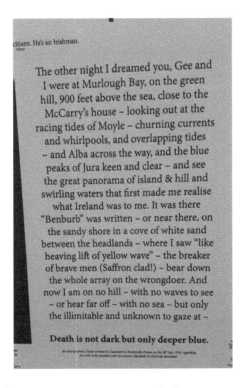

citizen. He's an Irishman.

The other night I dreamed you, Gee and I were at Murlough Bay, on the green hill, 900 feet above the sea, close to the McCarry's house – looking out at the racing tides of Moyle – churning currents and whirlpools, and overlapping tides – and Alba across the way, and the blue peaks of Jura keen and clear – and see the great panorama of island & hill and swirling waters that first made me realise what Ireland was to me. It was there "Benburb" was written – or near there, on the sandy shore in a cove of white sand between the headlands – where I saw "like heaving lift of yellow wave" – the breaker of brave men (Saffron clad!) – bear down the whole array on the wrongdoer. And now I am on no hill – with no waves to see – or hear far off – with no sea – but only the illimitable and unknown to gaze at –

Death is not dark but only deeper blue.

An excerpt from a letter written by Casement in Pentonville Prison on the 30th July 1916 regarding his wish to be reunited with his cousins, Elizabeth & Gertrude Bannister.

These words by Casement were next to the big cross near Fair Head.

Roger was born in Dublin but lived for quite a few years in Co. Antrim. After his hanging in 1916, he was buried in Pentonville Prison in London. His remains were eventually released by the British Government in 1965, only on the condition that they could not be brought into Northern Ireland. He had a State funeral in Dublin and was buried in Glasnevin Cemetery. So he never got his dying wish to have his body brought back to Murlough Bay.

After passing through an open gate, I took an immediate right which brought me up onto a grassy cliff-top trail called 'Grey Man's Path' (well named for the man climbing it today!)

Grey Man's Path on Fair Head, Co. Antrim

The weather is perfect now; no sign of any rain or wind with the sun shining through. Shortly I come to the very top of Fair Head (or Benmore). I'm also only about 20 km from the Scottish mainland (Mull of Kintyre) which I can easily see to the east.

These steep cliffs are now very popular with rock climbers. I see two small rucksacks with a rope tied around a big boulder and the rope dropping down the vertical cliff. I'm too scared to even get close to check if I can see the climbers!

These 'climbing cliffs' have been given their own names by the rock climbers. From east to west there's the 'small crag', 'main crag', 'farangandoo' and 'marconi's cove' which was only discovered in 1988. I don't think I've ever seen cliffs with such a vertical drop!

It's only about 4 km across to Rathlin Island now and it was on the Island that Robert the Bruce was inspired by a struggling spider to have the "tenacity to keep trying till it succeeds" (I'll heed this advice later!). Further north of Rathlin, I can even see the Scottish islands of Islay and Jura.

It's no surprise either that 'Game of Thrones' was filmed here and in fact in Season 7, this was the spot (here in Fair Head) where Jon Snow finally gets to meet the beautiful Daenerys Targaryen (probably the two most famous characters in Game of Thrones).

Rock bridge near Fair Head, Co. Antrim

So up to now, everything is going well on this beautiful day! However, it looks like 'grey man's path' has come to an end, and so I run further inland hoping to pick up the trail again. I come to a country road and to a farm entrance, but there's a 'Private Property' notice here.

I climb over a style on the other side of the road and try to follow a path, but it doesn't seem to lead to anywhere! I decide to backtrack all the way back to the coast again. Then I climb over a fence and eventually make it down to the shore. I think I see Marconi's Cottage in the distance. I figure I will have a nice run along the coast and soon I'll be in Ballycastle… but it's never that easy! The lower coastal path abruptly comes to an end, and so I have no alternative but to leave the coast, climb up a huge hill to try to find another trail.

Maybe I came too far inland as I end up having to run through a few fields and eventually (yes that word 'eventually' that never really explains how much I suffered!) I get back onto a narrow coastal cliff-path. Now I can see Marconi's cottage very clearly down on the shore.

Marconi's Cottage

This is where Marconi's employees made the first-ever wireless telegraph transmission in the world. It was between here and Rue Point on Rathlin (just about 5 km away). Marconi himself, the famous Italian inventor, only spent four days in this area, coincidentally for him, to coincide with the annual *'Old Lammas Fair'* in Ballycastle!

Marconi's Cottage (just outside Ballycastle, Co. Antrim)

I thought I could stay on this cliff path all the way to Ballycastle, but that also came to an abrupt end, so I struggle down the hill through high grass and tree ferns to finally get to Marconi's Cottage. I think if I was doing this run again, it might be easier starting in Ballycastle at Marconi's Cottage (there seems to be a path from the house) and doing this stretch to Fair Head with the sea on my left.

Anyway, I'm glad to be down on the shore again, and now I have a nice straight run in along the coast road. I soon get down onto the beach at Ballycastle, run along the strand and Maureen and the boys are there to meet me at the point where the Glenshesk River flows into the sea. Stage 12 is now completed in full.

STAGE 13:

❖

Co. Antrim: Ballycastle to Portrush

Saturday 10 Feb 2018

40 km or 25 miles

'Summer passes and one remembers one's exuberance. Winter passes and one remembers one's perseverance'. Yoko Ono

It might be spring according to the Celtic Calendar, but it still felt very cold this weekend. I must admit though I was looking forward to today's (Saturday's) stage, especially as I knew we would pass such famous and magical places along the Antrim coast.

We're now at the top of Ireland at Ballycastle (not surprisingly voted by Sunday Times readers as the nicest place to live in N.Ireland), and from now on we'll be heading west with the vast Atlantic Ocean on our north/right-hand side. First we travel to Portrush (today's finish destination) and to add to our agony this weekend, we decide first to run the Portrush parkrun (along a lovely stretch of sandy beach on the East Strand).

It's just the usual three of us today Helen, Sean and me. After we complete the parkrun we are grateful to Bob and Judith McLaughlin who drive us from Portrush to Ballycastle to begin Stage 13. Despite the forecast of showers (they'll come later!) it's quite a nice morning and Rathlin Island is gleaming in the sunshine across the bay as we leave Ballycastle at 11.05 am.

We don't normally like running on the road, but we have no alternative for the first few miles (although we do get a slight off-road loop through a narrow trail just after we leave Ballycastle). Later we emerge from one of our long hills climbs to see Sheep Island sitting majestically in the blue sea with the Rope Bridge clearly visible below us. Two Californian visitors stop to ask us for directions to the 'dark hedges', one of the many 'Game of Thrones' beauty spots in this area.

Even on a cold February day, there are quite a few tourists here heading to the Rope Bridge - some of them even cheer us on as we run by! The Rope-Bridge crosses from high cliffs on the Antrim coast to a tiny island. Salmon fishermen have been building bridges over to the island for over 350 years. The three of us pause in the middle of the rope bridge, trying not to look down! Fortunately for us, the shaky bridge has got safer over the years (even in the 1980s it had only one handrail and large gaps between the slats!)

Carrick-a-Rede Rope Bridge, Co. Antrim

We leave the Rope-bridge and find a lovely grassy path from Carrick-a-Rede to Ballintoy. Well it starts off grassy, but soon it turns into a very muddy path! Shortly we arrive in Ballintoy. It's over 20 years since I first came to magical Ballintoy (place of the axe) - such a beautiful secluded little harbour. No surprise at all that it was used for the fictional town of Lordsport in Game of Thrones.

Helen made me pose like this at beautiful Ballintoy harbour, Co. Antrim

We carry on along the coastal path (still muddy!), clamber over a few rocks and eventually come to the magnificent long sandy beach at White Park Bay. Then it's over a few more rocks until we join the coastal path at Portbradden (port of the salmon).

Gerry and Sean running along Whitepark Bay, Co. Antrim

We struggle on; passing Dunseverick harbour and Dunseverick Castle (not much of the castle left, but the location for the castle on the top of the cliff is spectacular!) We pass Port Moon where fishermen have harvested kelp, crabs, lobsters and salmon for centuries.

Of course Sean knows this route very well having completed the Causeway Coast marathon here. Helen and I struggle to keep up with him though and have to tip-toe through the mud.

We reach Benbane Head – the most northerly point in N.Ireland, although Malin Head in Donegal is geographically further north.

The sky is getting darker, and we carry along through the muddy (and hilly) coastal path. It's beginning to feel like a long day already. We continue along headland after headland, and soon the rain comes down. Although its light rain, it's relentless and we're beginning to feel a bit miserable by the time we arrive at a busy Giant's Causeway.

We don't delay too long at the famous Causeway as the rain gets heavier. We stop briefly at the Causeway hotel for a drink (only coke and water!). The TV is on, and I notice Ireland are beating Italy 42-0. Yes it would be nice to stop here in front of a warm fire with a pint of Guinness and watch the rest of the rugby!

We find another (muddy) coastal path outside the hotel, which leads us alongside a narrow gauge railway. This line is for a steam train that runs from the Giants Causeway to nearby Bushmills. We continue along the coast to Port Ballintrae and stop for coffee which warms us a little (coffee would have even been nicer with a drop of Bushmills!) and then we carry on through the rain for the last few miles.

We are delighted to see the ruins of Dunluce castle at last. Apparently years ago in the castle, part of the kitchen next to the cliff face collapsed into the sea, after which the wife of the owner refused to live there any longer.

We can now easily see those big rocks known as the Skerries, and its back down onto Portrush strand. Its 5.00 pm now; cold, wet and getting dark as we complete today's stage.

STAGE 14:

Portrush (Co. Antrim) to Benone (Co. Derry)

Sunday 11 Feb 2018

42 km or 26 miles

It's exactly one year to the day since we left Omeath in Co. Louth (Stage One) to start this whole adventure. If we thought the weather was bad yesterday, it was nothing compared to today. The snow, sleet and wind were persistent from early morning.

The good news was that we had three other brave runners joining us at 8.30 am in Portrush, Neill Weir, Laura Doherty and Jim Blee. Laura and Jim live in Portrush and are training for the Manchester marathon, and Neill is both an ultra runner and a 5 km specialist (and everything in between). Neill also became our driver later on.

The six of us leave the East Strand in Portrush and head west facing a cold and harsh head-wind. We follow the coast towards Portstewart town, taking the cliff path and arriving at Portstewart strand, which has the perfect sand for running on – not too soft and not too hard.

However, there are no *'red sails in the sunset'* today – that was the song written by Jimmy Kennedy in 1935 as he saw the yacht 'Kitty of Coleraine' sailing by as he walked along the beach. (At Portstewart we say goodbye to Neill - for a while anyway – but we are really glad to see him later!)

It was a tough two-mile run on the strand against the sleet and snow with very little protection from the elements. At the end of the Portstewart beach, we reach the River Bann and what is known as the Barmouth. The Bann really divides Northern Ireland in two, and here we are at the exact spot that the river flows into the sea. It seems like a short hop across to the other side at Castlerock, and it would be nice if there was some kind of footbridge here to continue our adventure along the Co. Derry coast. It turns out to be a 12-mile roundtrip to get to the other side at Castlerock!

Well earned coffee at the 10mile mark in Portstewart

So we head back along Portstewart beach again. At least we have the wind and sleet behind us this time! We stop briefly at Harry's Shack, get some takeaway coffees and share one scone between us! We continue along the road into Coleraine and cross the River Bann. At the bridge, we are very sad to say goodbye to Laura and Jim. They were brave to join us in such miserable conditions.

We take a right turn at Coleraine Grammar, along Ballycairn Road and another right into Cranagh Road which leads onto Ballywoollen Road. I read that when St Patrick arrived in this neighbourhood he was received with great honour and hospitality by the local chieftain, Nadslua. I don't think many of the locals even notice us as we soldier on through these quiet country roads.

Co. Derry – looking across to Inishowen in Donegal

Suddenly Helen gets all excited as we pass a place called Ardina. It turns out that her grandfather came from this area, and he never forgot his birthplace. Helen explained that when her granddad moved to Groomsport, Co. Down he even called his house Ardina **'I was born in Ardina and I'll die in Ardina'**, he said.

We continue along Ballywoolen road until we get to Springvale Lane. We take a right turn down towards Castlerock Golf Course, crossing the railway line on our way. There are absolutely no golfers on the course today – just as well maybe, as we trample through greens and fairways. We can hear the ocean now! We cross the sand dunes onto Castlerock Strand, and we have finally arrived on the other side of the Barmouth (just opposite Portstewart strand). We continue through Castlerock, and as we climb the hill in the village, that cold rain and sleet start to come down again!

We shortly join a coastal path along the cliff and are glad to see the iconic Mussenden Temple in the distance. As we get closer to the Temple, we notice that there's a vast bay of water in our way! It seems we have to walk down from the cliff, tackle another muddy treacherous path, cross a bridge and climb up a steep hill on the other side. We finally arrive tired, cold and miserable at Mussenden Temple.

Sean and Gerry in freezing cold at Mussenden Temple, Co. Derry

I don't think I've ever been as cold and I know Helen and Sean feel the same! My hands just can't get warm despite wearing gloves. It's a little bit easier if I close my hands in a fist inside the gloves. It's at this point that I suggest that we could finish earlier than originally planned. Helen and Sean agreed. The original plan was to run as far as Magilligan Point, another 5 miles or 8 km. Luckily Neill is already driving in this direction, so we arrange to meet him later in Benone, only 2 miles away. It's a long two miles to our finish line, and we are so delighted to get there. It's been a tough weekend. We've run 54 miles in miserable weather over the weekend (including parkrun), and now we're only one stage away from completing the whole N.Ireland coast.

STAGES 15:

❖

Co. Derry: Benone to Muff (Derry/Donegal border) via Magilligan

Saturday 10 March 2018

55 km or 34.2 miles

'I guess it comes down to a simple choice, really. Get busy living or get busy dying!'
(from Shawshank Redemption by Stephen King)

You can read later why I'm quoting from a prison drama, but I can't believe how well this whole adventure is going! I was so lucky to have two amazing athletes in Helen and Sean to share this mad idea with. Their personalities shone through even on the most miserable days, and they inspired me along the way. It was such a privilege to get to know them (so well!) over the last 13 months. However, since our last run, we've had some sad news with Helen losing her Dad. It's been a tough couple of weeks for Helen and her family.

As regards the weather, our miserable winter continues! Just last week we had 'Beast from the East' and 'Storm Emma' too. Today, I woke to a very wet morning. At least when we arrived in Benone, about 7.50 am, the rain was easing slightly. We were also worried about running on the Benone-Magilligan section of the strand as we had heard reports that the army had control of that part of the beach, and it can be a no-go area. Someone else had said that red flags would appear if the army were having firing practice!

Anyway we made our way down to Benone Strand and started running west towards Magilligan point.

There was a civil rights demonstration led by John Hume on this very beach just a few days before Bloody Sunday in January 1972. Video footage shows the famous Derry man confronting an army officer "tell your soldiers to stop firing rubber bullets'. The officer replies "this is a prohibited area". Mr. Hume asks the officer 'are you proud of the way your men are treating this crowd today". The officer just keeps replying that the beach 'is a prohibited area'. So yes, it did feel good today running on this restricted area.

Firing range on Magilligan beach, Co. Derry

We reach Magilligan Point, and now we're so close to Donegal. We can easily see Green-castle on the other side – just about a mile across – and Cnoc Alainn (beautiful moun-tain) behind.

On this great coastal adventure of ours, we often like to take part in a nearby parkrun, but it's still hard to believe that Helen, Sean and I actually did a parkrun today inside the pris-on walls of Magilligan! Of course Magilligan Prison has a long history in N.Ireland going back to the 1970s during Internment. Later in 1998, hundreds of prisoners were released as part of the Good Friday Agreement. Recently the prison has received an encouraging report 'the most positive ever about a jail in Northern Ireland' from the Criminal Justice Inspection. We had heard that there was a weekly parkrun inside Magilligan prison (at 9.30 am on Saturdays) called Lower Drummans parkrun and we were very keen to take part. There were complications with security etc, but we persevered, and we were eventually rewarded. There are a lot of campaigns to get people out of prison, but we had our own private campaign this week (led by Helen!) to get us into Magilligan prison! It was a surreal but amazing experience running around the six laps – on the day prisoners did all volunteering and marshalling.

Having completed parkrun at Magilligan prison, Co. Derry

On the way out we passed through the various security prison gates again, collected our phones and continued our adventure (strange to be running away from a prison!) Afterwards, we were still buzzing with excitement and hardly noticed that the rain had started again!

We had also hoped to run along Magilligan Strand, but after leaving the prison, we realised we were already a mile or two inland, so we decided to stay on the road. We passed the small village of Bellarena (beautiful strand). There's a brand new railway station there with two platforms. Bellarena is the last stop (before Derry) on the Belfast to Londonderry line as the route heads towards the coast. (I've never travelled by train in this area but it must be the most beautiful journey, especially on the Coleraine-Derry section).

About a mile after Bellarena station, we take a right turn onto a quieter road (B69). We cross over the River Roe, and after about five miles, we arrive on the outskirts of Limavady (leap of the dog). Limavady is most famous for the tune 'Londonderry Air' or 'Danny Boy' collected by Jane Ross in the mid-19th century from a local fiddle player. We're now back on the busy A2 again and stop briefly at a shop in Ballykelly for drinks and some hot cross buns (Sean is hungry again!). Helen is keen to keep going, and we continue on the A2 through Ballykelly Forest until we arrive in the village of Greysteel.

As we're running around the coast of Northern Ireland, we can't forget the horrific atrocities committed in recent years. On 30 October 1993 members of the UDA, a loyalist paramilitary group, opened fire on civilians in a crowded pub in Greysteel during a Halloween party, killing eight and wounding nineteen. The group claimed responsibility, saying the attack was revenge for Shankill Road bombing (another terrible atrocity) by the IRA, exactly a week earlier. In Greysteel one of gunman yelled "trick or treat" as he opened fire.

We can see a sign in the distance that we think says, 'Londonderry 6 miles' but as we get closer, we realise that it's actually 8 miles. I'm beginning to struggle now, and those extra two miles don't help!

Sean discovers a much quieter road that runs parallel to the A2 (Clooney Road by Longfield Estate), making it a little easier. I'm in a slow-running mode now as Helen and Sean power on ahead. It's a long, tough slog but eventually, we arrive in the outskirts of Derry City. We had talked about crossing the Peace Bridge, but that would have added another 4 miles to our journey. Instead we head for the Foyle Bridge, north of the city, which proved in itself, to be a long, long climb. Still it was a great feeling to reach the top of the bridge with views down into the city. (The bridge's span is the longest in the island of Ireland, at 234 metres.)

We cross the Foyle Bridge, having now completed 33 miles today - just 5 more miles to go! I eat the banana that I've been carrying since Ballykelly (many miles ago!). Sean keeps running and is keen to continue onto our finish point at Muff, (Derry/Donegal border). Helen quickly follows Sean, and I take up the rear again, keeping them both in sight in the distance.

Up to now, we had been lucky with the weather, nothing too bad and we were still quite dry. We had punished ourselves so much already today, but as we headed for the Donegal border, Mother Nature decided to put the boot in! Yes suddenly the heavens opened, and within a few minutes, we were soaked to the skin. The roads were getting flooded too and twice I was drenched by passing cars. I could just about make out Sean (through the heavy mist) in the distance. Helen was somewhere even further ahead.

Along with the heavy rain, the wind was now against us too. Still we persevered to the Donegal Border. In a bizarre and perverse kind of way it was the perfect weather to the end of our run around Northern Ireland.

PS. We are indebted once again to our hero, Neill Weir who drove us, early in the morning, to Benone Strand. He then ran a 10-mile race in Derry (finishing second in 53 minutes!), met us briefly at the Foyle Bridge, collected us at the border in Muff and took three 'drowned rats' to Foyle Arena for a nice warm shower. Thank you so much Neill.

Gerry Sean and Helen soaked to the skin at Derry-Donegal border

It was also the end of our Clifton Running Team (Helen, Sean and me) as we had reached the border. It was such an incredible feat for the three of us to complete the whole coast of Northern Ireland in just thirteen months. Although I started this journey (back in February 2017) with a hip injury, I was now feeling fit, and I was determined to complete the whole proper province of Ulster. It was understandable that Helen and Sean, with so many other things going on in their lives, couldn't join me. However, without them, I could have never had got this far.

Stage 15 – Revisited: Co. Derry: Magilligan Point to Ballymartin

Monday 13 July 2020

No extra mileage

I think the main reason why Helen, Sean and I missed this part of Magilligan Strand (east Foyle shore) in March 2018 was that we were just out of prison! Yes, we had just done the parkrun inside the prison, and we were already about a mile along the country road heading for Bellarena.

Anyway, back to today. It was an early start as I arrive at Magilligan Point at 7.30 am. I'm joined today by my friend and ex-neighbour Jeremy McLucas, and we're going to WALK along the coast (it's not always about running, you know!) It's a dull July morning and to use a good Galway phrase 'there's Rain on the Wind'.

Magilligan Point with Donegal only one mile across

Low tide is at 8.30 am – hence the early start. From here at Magilligan Point we can clearly see Greencastle in Donegal (only a mile across), and it's good to hear that the ferry is operating again.

After a short walk on the road, Jeremy and I get down onto a rocky shoreline (even at low tide it's not as sandy as the Ordnance Survey map suggests!) Speaking of Ordnance and Maps, I read that this area around Magilligan was originally used as a 'base line' in the 1820s for all maps in Ireland. This was because of the strand's flatness and its closeness to Scotland which had been mapped in previous decades. Looking at our map today we know there are ten or eleven streams to cross along this long stretch of coastline, and shortly we come to the first one.

This stream isn't that deep but at this early stage I don't want to get my shoes wet and so I walk barefoot for a while (Jeremy is more prepared with proper waterproof shoes!) As we gradually crossed stream after stream, none of them were as wide as the first one. It probably helped though that we tackled this stretch of the coast at low tide.

Crossing first of many streams just south of Magilligan Point

We don't meet anyone along this part of the coastline, but we do see an old abandoned car on the beach!

Jeremy checking out Capri or maybe Rover!

Our original plan was to leave the coast at Scotchtown Road (after crossing all the streams) and then come back onto the main road. However, Jeremy suggested we carry on walking along the coast, through a grassy path and field as far as the river Roe where the railway bridge crosses over.

Even at low tide, the River Roe would be difficult to cross (too deep and too wide). Instead we make our way up onto the railway bridge. Very cautiously, we watch, look and listen to make sure there are absolutely no trains coming and then we quickly cross over the railway bridge. Warning: Please be very careful here! We checked beforehand the times of the train (it was a bank holiday too) and we quickly crossed over the river, making sure not to delay in any way along the railway line.

We still felt relieved to be on the other side, and despite the light rain, we stopped to have a deserved break. The good thing about walking is it's much easier to carry food!

Nice trail just south of River Roe

On this side of the river, we had the option of varying our walk, sometimes along the narrow wall by the sea (Ballymacran/Ballykelly bank) or later on the nice country trail below. There were lovely views now across to the hills at Bienvenagh (looks a bit like Ben Bulben in Sligo). We passed lovely lush green grass.

Jeremy and I at Bienveagh near Ballykelly

Jeremy pointed out that this grass is grown by a company called Emerald Lawns. You can buy lawns here and get it delivered to your door the next day! This whole area was once a dense forest (Jeremy informs me), and the building of the Ballykelly bank in the 1840s meant that thousands of acres were reclaimed from the sea.

We cross over a small bridge (Burnfoot river) and continue. The sun is even making an appearance now, and it's a very pleasant walk.

There was also an RAF airport nearby which was an important base for anti-submarine aircraft in WW2. A plane crashed into the shallow waters here in 1944, and even today Jeremy and I could still see the remains of that aircraft in the sea. Luckily, the Canadian pilot, although badly injured, survived the crash. (earlier that year, nine Airmen were not so lucky when their plane crashed in the nearby Bienvenagh hills.)

We leave the coast and head inland, and shortly we have reached our finish line in the village of Ballykelly. Jeremy's wife, Tiffany, meets us there (and after nice coffee and buns!) she kindly drives us back to Magilligan Point.

PS: Our walk today was 21 km or 13 miles (we didn't actually make up any extra miles compared to my original run on country roads back in March 2018).

STAGE 16:

❖

Co. Donegal: Muff to Culdaff

Saturday 14 April 2018

56 km or 34.8 miles

Remember to look up at the stars and not down at your feet
(Stephen Hawking RIP 14/3/2018)

Me with Brian and Maureen (disguised as Sean and Helen!)

I'm on my own now. Helen and Sean have other adventures and commitments, and in my wisdom, I've decided to continue alone into Donegal to try to complete the WHOLE province of Ulster. I can't thank Helen and Sean enough for getting me this far. Together we've covered 663 km (412miles) of Northern Ireland coastline. I know this is a mad decision (by me!) to continue into Donegal, but here I am with my wife Maureen and son Brian at the Derry/Donegal border on a pleasant April morning. Maureen had kindly offered to drive me to Muff (at the border), and the plan was that we'd meet later in Culdaff where we're staying the night. Well, it didn't quite go as planned but more about that later! It's the longest Winter I ever remember, but it's a beautiful spring morning today in east Donegal as I begin my coastal journey around the Inishowen Peninsula.

I realise I have to run on a fairly busy road for the first 20 km until I reach Moville. At least for most of the way, the road is wide, and there's a kind of off-road mud trail that I can run on. As I get near to Quigley's Point, I've got lovely Lough Foyle closely on my right-hand side.

It's about 11.00 am as I arrive in Moville (or 'Bun an Phobail', which means 'foot of the Foyle'). I stop to buy a bottle of water and slowly walk through the town.

Yes I'm definitely in Donegal. Moville, Inishowen

I continue running north and follow the coast road to Greencastle. There's a coastal walk that takes me off the road at Greencastle (by the way this was the third Greencastle I've passed on my coastal journey so far). I decide to head down to the beach at the strangely named, 'Eleven Ballyboes'. The tide is out fully now so I can run along the strand for a while. I have to come back onto the country road again, and after a few miles, I arrive at Stroove/Shroove Lighthouse and the beautiful beach at Cornashamma Bay.

I get chatting to a German couple who are having a picnic beside their camper van. They tell me they're doing the Wild Atlantic Way. "*So am I*", I say and explain exactly what I'm doing. They think I'm crazy and suggest that I should get a bicycle! I admire the sculpture 'Sruibh Brain' (or Sroove Bran) which depicts a rough sea crossing hundreds of years ago. Apparently this is the exact place where Saint Columba (Colmcille) left Ireland on his way to the island of Iona.

With a German couple I met

It's a long, tough climb at the beginning of the Inishowen Head Walk (or Loop as it's called). Eventually the narrow road up the hill turns into a rough trail. It's so quiet now. Although I've got the sea closely on my right-hand side (as always!), I'm at quite a high altitude. There's no wind, no rain and there's a pleasant warm sun on my back. The Inishowen Loop itself is a trail that rewinds its way down to the Lighthouse, so I have to be careful that I leave the Loop when I get to the top at Glenane Hill. It's about 1.15 pm now, and so far today everything has gone perfectly!

Eventually I make my way down closer to the sea towards the top of the cliff. It seems easier to walk here, but there are trees near the cliff edge, which hinder my progress. I can see Kinnagoe Beach so clearly in the distance now, but I'm way up on the cliff top with trees and bushes blocking any advancement. It's such a steep cliff too, and I have to be careful as I struggle along to find my way out. I seem to be trapped up here in the hills, with no clear way ahead! It's the first time today that I've missed my fellow coastal runners Helen and Sean! I'm sure they would figure a way out. Kinnagoe Bay seems so close, but it's so hard to get there! I spot a stone wall in the distance, and when I eventually reach it and climb over it, I see a flock of sheep that start to bleat like crazy at my presence. Yes I've finally reached civilization (a farmer's field). I run through a couple of fields and the farmer himself, having heard all the commotion, comes to greet me.

Kinnagoe Bay - La Trinidad Valencera (Spanish Armada)

As I'm running along the coast, I'm always conscious of people who've come this way before. I'm thinking of those Spanish soldiers who perished (either at sea or later as they arrived inland) in 1588. After a failed battle against the English to overthrow Elizabeth First and Protestantism, the Spanish Armada fled north along the east coast of England and Scotland and attempted to navigate Ireland's north and west. Due to terrible weather and primitive navigation charts, many of the ships crashed against the Irish coast. One of their main ships, La Trinidad Valencera, came into Kinnagoe and sunk here in the bay. It was almost 400 years later before the ship's remains were eventually discovered in 1971 by members of the City of Derry Sub Aqua Club.

Kinnagoe Bay where Spanish Armada Boat crashed

It was reported that when Philip II of Spain learned of the disastrous result of the Armada expedition, he declared,

"I sent the Armada against men, not God's winds and waves".

Anyway, back to April 2018. At this stage, I was still exhausted after my earlier exploits in the hills. It now seemed a long way down to Kinnagoe Bay and anyway I had seen enough of that beach from the cliff top. So in my wisdom, after I left the farm, I decided to stay up on a higher road and head directly to Culdaff. This was a big mistake, and yes, I could have done with Helen and Sean again at this stage! That higher road I was on was not taking me to Culdaff. It was taking me back to Greencastle, where I had reached about 2 hours ago! It took me a while to realise this. It was now 3.00 pm, I had run 46 km already today, and I was back near the spot I had reached about noon earlier. (so just like the Spanish Armada - bad navigation was to blame!)

Culdaff, Inishowen, Donegal

I couldn't believe what had happened. At Kinnagoe Bay, I was only 11 km from my finish point at Culdaff. I should have been arriving at 3.00 pm in Culdaff as initially planned. I was so upset at this stage, really felt like abandoning the whole adventure. I decided (eventually) to ring Maureen, and she kindly came to meet me.

I finally make it to Kinnagoe beach

I suppose the good news was that I was only 11 km away from Culdaff when I took that fatal wrong turn. Maureen, Brian, and I stayed the night in Culdaff (with the Lynch's at Ceecliff B&B), and Maureen encouraged me to complete that 11 km stretch on the following morning. So I decided to get up early (before breakfast) to complete the Culdaff-Kinnagoe section of Stage 16. For this one occasion, I kept the sea on my left-hand side! Maureen and Brian followed me later in the car, and I finally made it to Kinnagoe Beach to properly complete Stage 16.

STAGE 17:

❖

Co. Donegal: Culdaff to Ballyliffen (via Malin Head)

Friday 4th May 2018

69.8 km or 43.4 miles

"And fair are the valleys of Green Inishowen and hardly the fishers that call them their own"

Although I still miss the company of Helen and Sean, I'm blessed with some lovely weather as I leave the lovely village of Culdaff on the Inishowen Peninsula. Heading north along the 'Inishowen 100', I pass Portaleen and then I have to come inland as there is no coastal path (just high cliffs!) on this (north east) side of Inishowen. After about four miles of running inland, I take a right turn at the T junction and another right after two miles leads me back down towards the shore and to the beautiful Malin Well.

At the coast at Malin Well, there are huge rock formations in this secluded top corner of Inishowen. You can easily see why the recent Star Wars film was shot in this area. (Star Wars addicts will enjoy the fact that today is actually May the fourth!!)

View from Ruins of Church at Malin Well

It's so peaceful here on my own, and I pause for a while at the Grotto and Church ruins and at the 'Wee House of Malin' where a hermit once lived in a cave. I wonder what possesses someone to run off on their own like that!!

I follow the coast with Malin Head clearly visible now and carry on along a lovely grassy stretch (perfect for running on) for a good half mile. At the end of the grassy section, I take a rough trail inland that takes me back up onto the country road (the 'Inishowen 100').

I come to a T junction after a while and take a right towards Malin Head. When I reach Malin Head itself, there's a bit of a hill to run up. I can see a group of tourists at the top watching me suffer, but when I reach the top they cheer me on!

So I'm now at the top of Ireland – the most northerly point! It's called Banba's Crown, after Banba who was one of the mythical queens of Ireland. I walk down to the edge of the cliff at Malin Head and see huge letters spelling out the word EIRE formed from placing stones together. I notice as I got close that the stones are all cemented together. They've been here since World War 2, and it was to signify to passing planes that Ireland was a neutral country during the war.

EIRE sign at top of Malin Head to signify Irish WW2 Neutrality

At Main Head, I even get to enjoy some water and coffee. When I ask directions from the man at the coffee stand, he tells me I have lots of hills to climb, but he says in all seriousness 'at least you can free-wheel down the other side'. I look at him and say 'you know I'm just running, not cycling'. 'Oh' he says, I thought you were on a bike!

I leave Malin Head and continue around the top corner of Ireland, so I'm now heading south! On this west side of Inishowen, it's much easier to get to the shore, and at White Strand Bay I make my way down to the beach and run along this sometimes rocky beach for a few miles. My way becomes impaired as I'm running alongside a wide stream. Eventually I come to a wee bridge, and I'm happy to join up with the 'Inishowen 100' country road again.

I stop to talk to a few French tourists from La Rochelle and continue on this quiet but hilly section. It's brightening up now, and soon I reach a beautiful viewing point overlooking the spectacular Five Fingers beach. I follow the road downhill, take a right turn at a crossroads and right again at the church and reach the amazing Five Fingers (Lagg) strand. This beach was voted in the top 25 beaches in Ireland and best for 'Solitude' which was very apt as I was the only person on the beach.

Five Fingers (Lagg) Strand in Inishowen, Donegal

I continue along the beach, come back onto the main road again, and soon come to Malin town where I stop for a water drink and follow the Carndonagh road. After about 3 km, I took a right turn (signposted to 'Driving Test Centre' and so avoiding Carndonagh).

I'm exhausted at this stage. I'm walking, running and walking again! I come back on the main road, take a right towards Ballyliffin, and after about 5 km I take a right again into Doagh Island (or Isle of Doagh).

The isle of Doagh was once an island, but the channel silted up over time and became joined to the mainland. This detour of mine of about 12 km to circle the island was well worth it. Doagh (pronounced 'Doe') had plenty to keep me entertained with spectacular scenery, standing stones, signs and stories explaining the origin of various houses/townlands and a Famine village of thatched cottages. Even when I eventually circle the whole 'island' I have the beautiful Pollan Strand to run on with the sea on my right and the wide beach (lucky for me the tide is out) and Golf Links on my left. The Irish Open Golf Championship is taking place here in Doagh/Ballyliffin this summer. It's the perfect location and the ideal place to finish my longest coastal run so far.

STAGE 18:

❖

Co. Donegal: Ballyliffin to Buncrana

Saturday 5th May 2018

36.5 km or 22.7 miles

I leave Lynch's at Ceecliff Guesthouse in Culdaff after a nice breakfast (poached eggs and smoked salmon) and drive to Ballyliffin. I'm not sure if it was a good idea running at all today after my 70 km run yesterday – yes 43 miles - and definitely the longest I've ever run in my life! I suffered today! It's slightly cool as I head off from Ballyliffin and very shortly (after about 3 km) I arrive in the village of Clonmany.

Clonmany

This village has been unlucky with freak weather in the past. In 1840, the village experienced an earthquake. The Belfast Newsletter reported that "some people were thrown from their chairs, and greatly alarmed." Then as recently as August 2017, the village was severely affected by flooding. Some residents were cut off due to rising river levels and had to be rescued from their homes.

I saw these abandoned shoes on posts at Tullagh Point (previous Coastal Runner calling it a day maybe?)

I head for the coast again as far as Tullagh Point and continue through the townland of Dunaff, and I take a right at the Post Office. This brings me on to a perfect coastal country road which eventually turns into a nice downhill rough track that takes me all the way to Lenan Pier. Fanad Head is clearly visible on the other side of Lough Swilly.

At Lenan Bay I'm tempted to follow a rough coastal road and track over the Urris Hills. However, looking at the Ordnance Survey Map, the track seems to disappear half way over the mountain. This coastal route would definitely be a much shorter way to reach Crummiest Bay and Dunree Head. After my exploits of struggling through Inishowen Head in April, I'm reluctant to cross over rough terrain, although this coastal route looked very achievable on a day like today.

The other reason I don't take this rough coastal way today is that I'm hoping to meet up with Helen and Neill. Helen (fellow coastal runner as far as Derry/Donegal border) and Neill are cycling today around the Inishowen peninsula. I know they're going to have to come over the Gap of Mamore and I'm really looking forward to meeting them. In fact that idea of meeting them is giving me great motivation to keep going. I leave Lehan Bay and head inland to get to the foot of Mamore Gap. It's a long steep climb up to the top. For cyclists, it's the steepest climb in Ireland. The maximum gradient is 22%, and even the average is 12.4%. I decide to walk!

There's amazing views all the way up here, and at the top of Mamore Gap there's a small grotto and well called Saint Colmcill's Well (or Saint Egney's Well.) There have been pilgrimages to this Well as far back as the 6th Century.

I descend from Mamore Gap. I'm still looking out for Helen and Neill (cycling Inishowen '100') but I know I can't miss them as they have to come over the 'Gap' too. I try to run down the steep hill, but even that's painful, and I have to walk again. I get to the bottom of the hill at the road junction and sit on the bridge (on the river Owenerk) and wait. Suddenly in the distance, I can hear Helen shouting 'Gerry, Gerry', and I spot two cyclists coming up the road from the coast.

It's really made my day to meet them, and the three of us stop for a while by the bridge in the sunshine.

Helen and Neill tackle Mamore Gap

After Helen and Neill left, I really struggled to run. Yesterday's 70 km run has taken its toll! I told my legs so many times to lift and move, but they refused to obey me!

Still the road down towards the coast at Dunree Head was amazing with magnificent views over the sea and across to Portsalon, with Ballymastocker Strand stretching out and smiling in the sunshine!

At this stage I'm struggling to keep up with these two!

I probably ended up walking almost all of the last 10 km to Buncrana. Nevertheless, I've been so lucky with the weather yesterday and today and to finish I have a nice path along the beach and shore in Buncrana.

I've now conquered the whole coast of Inishowen without even getting wet!

STAGE 19:

❖

Co. Donegal: Buncrana to Letterkenny

Saturday 9 June 2018

51.2 km or 31.8 miles

*'What does it mean, Donegal', I asked. 'Dun na nGall, fort of the foreigners'.
'But how are we foreigners when we live here'. (from 'The Bread Man' by Frank
McGuinness)*

The weather has been exceptionally good over the last few weeks, and today was no different even if the sun didn't shine. I set off from Donegal's second largest town, Buncrana
(means 'bottom of the river Crana') and head south towards Donegal's first largest town
Letterkenny (means 'hillside of the O'Cannons'). As usual I've got the sea on my right-hand
side and today the sea is Lough Swilly or 'Lake of the Shadows', as its sometimes called.

Buncrana

Buncrana is a lovely little town with one beach right behind the town and another beach
(The White Strand) which stretches about three miles south almost all the way to Inch
Island. The most famous person from Buncrana is probably the writer Frank McGuinness. He was still only 32 when he wrote the play 'Observe the Sons of Ulster Marching
towards the Somme'. Written in the middle of the Troubles in 1985 the play was praised
'because its author, a Republican Catholic dared to put himself imaginatively in the boots
of Ulster Unionist soldiers in the First World War'. McGuinness himself would say that

the play is really about 'the terror and horror of war'. To my knowledge, Frank McGuinness is the first and only honorary freeman of Buncrana. Wolfe Tone, one of the founders of the United Irishmen would not have happy memories of Buncrana. After he was captured off the Donegal coast on board a French Ship in 1798, he was at first unrecognised in French uniform, but later betrayed by an old friend, Sir George Hill.

Anyway I leave Buncrana along the main Derry/Letterkenny road, but I quickly get down onto the 'White Strand'. After a mile or two on the beach, there are large rocks and the sea has come in so I have to briefly come up onto Buncrana Golf Links. Not too many golfers around so I can easily run along the edge of the course. I'm quickly down on the sandy beach again, even if it's very soft sand – not great for the feet of the runner! Eventually I do have to leave the beach and run on the main road but only for about two miles until I reach the turnoff for Inch Island.

Inch Island

It's hard to even imagine that there was a railway station here (Inch Road Railway Station at Magherabeg) which operated from 1864 until 1948. The old 'Swilly' train ran along here in remote Donegal for over 80 years. I have to confess that I didn't actually circle Inch island. I got my bearings slightly wrong and ended up just hugging the SE corner of the island. After arriving onto the island itself, there was a lovely board walk to the left, through the forest which led to a trail, then directly onto Farland Causeway and back to the mainland on the south side of the island. (PS. I did go back – see later - to complete the whole island)

It was perfect weather for running (definitely no rain again today!) At this stage, all was well, but of course, not all goes to plan on this great coastal adventure!

Farland Causeway - leaving Inch Island

As I crossed the Causeway, leaving Inch Island, I checked my Ordnance Survey map which told me I could take a right turn after I arrived on the mainland and so I did take a right turn! The trail suddenly came to an abrupt end with only farmer's fields ahead, so I decided to head back the way I came. At this stage, I noticed some cows in the field getting very excited at my presence. There were 10 or 12 of them on the other side of the fence, and they started running in the same direction I was running. I slowed down but the cows didn't. They kept running in the field and eventually broke through a gate ahead of me and came out onto the track. I stayed back and was relieved to see the cows sprinting on ahead along the track and not towards me!

Anyway I had to come back onto the main Buncrana-Letterkenny road. It's a busy road on a Saturday afternoon, but after only about 2 km, I was able to leave the main road (at Black Bridge) again and head right towards the coast. I took the next left turn and headed in the direction towards Grange Causeway, which I knew would bring me even closer to the coast. From my Ordnance Survey map, I could see that the old Swilly railway line used to cross over Grange Causeway.

I carried on, climbing a fairly steep hill and at the top, I met a farmer (his name was Stanley, I found out later), and I asked *is this the way to the Causeway?'* 'No', he replied and said I should go back down the hill again. I ran down the hill took a left turn and after about a mile asked another man 'is the Causeway this way?' "Which Causeway are you looking for", he asked. I took out my map and explained that I had come from Inch Island and that I was now heading for the other causeway (I didn't know it was called Grange Causeway then).

'Ah, Grange Causeway', he said. He started to give me directions, and I then realised that the farmer, Stanley had sent me the wrong way! I eventually got back up the hill (after a sheep traffic jam delayed me even further!) and who did I meet at the top of the hill but again Stanley, the farmer at the same spot. *'You sent me on a wild goose chase'* I said. 'Oh', he said, 'I should have asked you which causeway-I thought you wanted to cross the causeway at Inch Island'. I told him I'd thank him some day, but not today! In the end, we both laughed about it!

With Stanley - I wasn't happy with him earlier!

Shortly afterwards I arrived at Grange Causeway (I had to take a dirt track through a slightly wooded area, so it's hard enough to find), However, the Causeway was worth waiting for, and it was a lovely run across the sea on a perfect grassy surface on such a beautiful day. I can only imagine how amazing it must have been to take the 'Swilly' train along here

Grange Causeway where 'Swilly' Train crossed until 1953

After leaving Grange Causeway, I followed the road for about 2 km through Ballybegly and onto a nice quiet country coastal road that eventually brought me back on the main road just outside Manorcunningham.

At Manorcunningham I decided to take a quieter inland route. After a while, I crossed over the main N14 road and then saw a sign for a Cycle Route into Letterkenny. I followed the cycle lane (really the old road) all the way into Letterkenny, running and walking (up those steep hills!). It was about 2.45 pm when I arrived in Letterkenny (still plenty of time before my 4.40 bus back to pick up my car at Buncrana).

Stage 19 – Revisited: Co. Donegal: Inch Island

Sunday 20 January 2019

11.6 km or 7.2 miles

On this coastal adventure, I've taken a wrong turn once or twice and I knew I didn't complete Inch Island properly. So on Sunday 20th January 2019, over 7 months later, I went back with Johnny McGrath and made sure I covered the whole island this time.

House and boat at Mill Bay, Inch island, Co. Donegal

Johnny, me and Francis Doherty at Inch island, Donegal

Johnny and I had just done Stage 26 on the day before (Sat 19 Jan 2019) and on our way back from Falcarragh, we stopped off at Inch Island. We drove onto Inch island and then to Mill Bay beach, which was our starting point for our circle run around the island. We decided to run clockwise for a change and took a turn left signposted to Binalt. Lots of hills on Inch island and it was a tough climb on the first few until we reached Binalt, where the country road comes to an abrupt end. We climbed over a gate and after a while another gate and another one and another one. We were running on a trail which gradually faded away. However, Johnny was able to find the path again even though it had become overgrown with bushes. We were joined along here by a few sheep, and eventually, the rough path brought us back onto the country road just beside Inch Pier. At a crossroads, we stop for a while to chat with a fellow runner, Francis Doherty. Ironically it was the Dohertys who settled on Inch Island and the castle on the south side of the island was built by the Doherty Clann. After another couple of miles, we finally arrive back at where we started at Mill Bay beach. Stage 19 now completed in full!

STAGE 20:

———— ❖ ————

Co. Donegal: Letterkenny to Portsalon

Sat. 30 June 2018

50.6 km or 31.4 miles

'I'm happy to be back again and greet you big and small - for there's no place on earth like the homes of Donegal' *Paul Brady*

It's a great summer so far and so warm this week! I had been keeping an eye on the weather all week, hoping it would cool down. However, despite the early start, it was still almost 20 degrees when I started today's run from Letterkenny at 8.07am. I had convinced Maureen (and Brian) to leave Bangor early (at 5.45 am). Such a beautiful morning and yes, as Paul Brady sings 'there's no place on earth like Donegal'.

None of these coastal runs go to plan (that's why it's called an adventure!) Each stage usually offers a different and unique challenge. Today the challenge was getting out of Letterkenny and finding the proper coastal route! I knew I had to follow the Ramelton/ Rathmelton road for a little while and then take a right turn at Barn Hill (Golf Course), bringing me down towards the coast. After about 10 km I came to the coast and to the ruins of Killydonnell Friary.

Killydonnell Friary, near Letterkenny and remains of Bishop O'Boyles chapel

This was the perfect place to stop. No sign of anyone around and aptly, I feel a bit like a hermit here at the friary. I read on a stone that one of my 'ancestors', Bishop Neal O'Boyle held a chapel here in these beautiful peaceful surroundings overlooking Lough Swilly. Also it was here that Calvagh O'Donnell and his wife were captured and taken into captivity by the famous Shane O'Neill. These O'Donnells were Shane's parent's in-law, and he later went on to marry his own mother-in-law! I suppose he captured her in more ways than one! I was getting so thirsty now! I stopped to talk to some cyclists, and they gave me a few sips of their water. I carried on, taking a right at a T junction and eventually after another 5 km reach Ballylin Point. Looking at this on the map (the night before) I was slightly concerned when I saw that the road came to an abrupt end, but I knew if I could get down onto the shore, I could join another country road (Ballylin Road) that would bring me into Ramelton. Lucky for me, I met a friendly face here. Her name was Helen (yes another Helen!). We chatted for a while outside her house, and she gave me a glass of water, which was much appreciated.

I was then able to run along the shore for about 500 metres until I joined up with the Ballylin Road. I followed this road for about 5 km, and at a T junction I was glad to see a sign saying, 'Ramelton 2 km.'

In Ramelton I crossed over the bridge on the river Leannan, and I was given some good news when I saw the sign saying 'Rathmullen 9 km'. To be honest, in this heat, I wasn't sure if I could make it all the way to Portsalon today, but the 9 km to Rathmullan seemed achievable.

Except it wasn't only 9 km to Rathmullan! I ran for about 1 km and then I passed a sign that said Rathmullan was now 10 km. After a while I passed another sign, still saying 10 km! You can imagine how glad I was to meet Maureen and Brian in Rathmullan. They had already got the ferry across and back to Buncrana. It was now 12.30 pm and still getting warmer.

In Rathmullan in 1607, the O'Neills and O'Donnells (the last of the Gaelic Order) left for the Continent. The Plantation of Ulster followed shortly afterwards. A beautiful sculpture depicts this defining moment in Irish history. Everything changed in Ireland after this.

I sit with Maureen and Brian for a while, eat a few salty skinny chips and drink lots more water. To be honest, at this stage, I'm not too enthusiastic about moving again. The beautiful beach in Rathmullan stretches for a few miles. Families, young and old, are enjoying a perfect day on the beach. A mad runner (yes me!) runs along the beach. Yes I know I keep saying 'sand is for the feet of the runner' but in this weather, I'm not so sure! It's now 27 degrees at 1.00 pm – Donegal is the warmest place in Ireland today!

Brian with mad runner on Rathmullan beach

There's very little traffic on this road to Portsalon. However as I get closer to Portsalon the hills are getting steeper. There are lovely views across the blue sea to Dunree Head in Inishown, and I can easily see the twisting cliff top road along the side of the Urris Hills (this was part of stage 18). The road is getting stickier too as the tar macadam begins to melt with the heat. I notice the cows in the fields are sitting down under trees – they've got the right attitude (no danger of cows running after me today!) I see a man in his parked car and ask him for a drink; he apologies that he doesn't have anything for me. I struggle through a few more hills, and then I hear a car beep behind me. I'm so pleased that it's Maureen and Brian. As I run around the next corner, I see Maureen has parked the car and behind her over the cliff is the most amazing sight!

I took this picture just as I arrived in Portsalon, Fanad, Co. Donegal.

It's Ballymastocker Strand in all its glory – so I've more or less arrived in Portsalon (port of the salt). I gulp down a few more pints of water and Maureen, Brian and I admire the spectacular view.

A few years ago the Observer Newspaper voted Stocker beach the second best beach in the world. Someone commented *'how was it ever pipped by some old Seychelles beach'*!

So to complete Stage 20, I just have a simple run downhill to this beautiful beach. I couldn't have asked for a better finish line or better place for cooling down afterwards.

STAGE 21:

Co. Donegal: Portsalon to Ballyheernan Bay

Monday 2 July 2018

21.4 km or 13.3 miles

M aureen suggested that I do this shorter stage while we were in Donegal, so I actually ran this stage clockwise with the sea on my left-hand side for a change.

Fanad Lighthouse, Co. Donegal

So I start stage 21 by taking a left turn from Fanad Lodge following the course of the road for a few hundred metres until I came to Eelburn Caravan park where I was able to run through a trail that brought me down onto a nice beach (Carrickachurdin Bay). I run along the beach for about 1 km until it came to an end and then take a trail which eventually brings me back to the main road and all the way to Fanad Lighthouse! The Lighthouse was voted the world's 2nd most beautiful lighthouse after Lindau Lighthouse in Germany (so just like Stocker Strand, another second in the world!). Maureen, Brian and I had got a really interesting tour of the Lighthouse the day before, but on this Monday morning, as I arrived, it was equally appealing. It was originally built in 1817 following numerous shipping disasters in this area, especially the HMS Saldanha in 1812. (see later)

So I leave the Lighthouse and backtrack (uphill!) for about 2 km until I came to the coastal road L1072 (Wild Atlantic way) to Portsalon where I take a left, keeping the sea on my left-hand side! The weather is cooler and much more pleasant today. It's quite hilly on this coastal route to Portsalon, but I'm determined to run up every single hill. I think the break I had yesterday did help and I've got my second wind today. It doesn't seem to take that long before I can see the magnificent Stocker Strand in the distance.

Heading towards Portsalon from north Fanad I quickly reach Portsalon Pier, and I stop for the first time since I left Fanad Lighthouse. This pier area has shops, cafe and a small secluded beach. I order another bottle of water and finish it quickly before heading off again.

HMS Saldanha Disaster

The last sighting of the Saldanha Ship was at 9.00 pm in December 1812. With violent storms, it hit the rocks at Carrickadonnel and 'became engulfed in the swirling surf of Ballymastocker Bay'. On the following morning, the beach was littered with over two hundred bodies and debris from the ship.

I took this photo just after arriving on Ballystocker Beach. Unfortunately for the crew on the Saldanha in 1811 it was completely different weather conditions for them.

Apparently a parrot was the only survivor on the ship, and he was shot shortly afterwards by a local farmer who didn't realise where this strange bird came from. There are reminders of the Saldanha and its crew all around this area, but the real (practical) memory to those who died is the Fanad Lighthouse built in 1817.

Path from Portsalon Pier to Portsalon beach

I discover a grassy path that goes from Portsalon Pier to the Golf Club which leads me down to the beach. What a finish I have in front of me! I still have about 3 km to go, but Ballymastocker strand was definitely made for the feet of the runner!

The tide is in fully now, but it's still easy enough to run on the beach. And to cap it all, Maureen and Brian are there to greet me again on this beautiful beach on the perfect summer's morning.

STAGE 22:

Co. Donegal: Circle of North West Fanad

Sat 25 Aug 2018

35.4 km or 22 miles

I'm back again in the Fanad Peninsula, although sometimes it's hard to know where Fanad starts and finishes. Back in 1835, the writer John O'Donovan stated "the natives around Rathmullan and Ramelton, who considered themselves civilised, deny that they themselves are men of Fanad". So, I'm definitely in 'uncivilised' Fanad today.

I think I'm recovering from my knee injury and have seen two different physios since my last run. Maybe it's a sign of ageing as I've also turned 60 since last month's adventure!

The sun is shining, but there's none of the heat like we had in June and July. Perfect weather for running! So I begin stage 22 by taking a left turn from Fanad Lodge, following the course of the road for about 200 hundred metres until I came to Eelburn Caravan park where I'm able to run through a trail that brought me down onto Ballyheernan beach. This time I take a left when I reach the strand (keeping the sea on my right-hand side of course!)

What a lovely start to today's run. The tide is out, so there's perfect sand for running on for about 1 km. Even when I leave the beach I continue onto a quiet country road/lane. After a while, I'm hoping to get down onto Donaghmore strand on the west coast of Fanad but I can't see any access as the farms seem to be fenced off.

Eventually I come to another junction in front of a lake. Luckily for me at this point, I meet a friendly farmer. I take out my map, and he explains exactly where I am. I'm standing right in front of Lake Naglea, and he advises me to take a right turn. I continue following this country road, passing Feighan Hill (apt name – yes another feckin hill!). However, the steep climb is worth it with magnificant views from the top across to the beaches on Rosguill Peninsula with the hill of Crocknasleigh clearly visibly across the bay.

View from Fanad peninsula across to Rosguill peninsula, Co. Donegal

I follow this quiet country road (no traffic at all!), eventually passing the sign for the Harry Blaney bridge. I continue straight, passing by Leat Beg Church and then I get a glimpse of the new bridge down in the valley to my right. The bridge opened in 2008 and crosses over Mulroy Bay from Fanad to Carrickart. It's named after Harry Blaney, an independent politician who secured its construction by supporting the Fianna Fail Government in 1997. It cost 20 Million Euro to build. Some critics have called it 'the bridge to nowhere', but after spending two days in Fanad and speaking to some of the locals, I've realised how the bridge has opened up life on the peninsula and connected people from Fanad to Carrickart, Creeslough and even west Donegal.

The Blaney Bridge connecting Fanad to west Donegal

I carry on running east towards Milltown (Baile an Mhuilinn) and then head north passing Tulaigh na Dala. Crossing over Bullock Bay to Kindrum, I finally arrive back again at Fanad Lodge where I'm spending the night. Stage 22 now completed.

STAGE 23:

—————— ❖ ——————

Co. Donegal: Ballyheernan Bay to Carrickart, via Millford.

Sunday 26 Aug 2018

39.2 km or 24.3 miles

The forecast for today was rain and more rain and it did pour a lot during the night. However it had stopped when I left Fanad Lodge at 10.00 am. Today's run was really along the main road which was quiet enough at this time of the morning, but as the day went on, there were more cars on the road. I carried on all the way to Millford (also known as Baile na nGalloglach/Gallowglass). I had planned to stop there, but there was a kind of 'by-pass' which put me on the road to Carrickart... so like Forrest Gump, I just kept running!

It's quite a wooded area just north of Millford, and it was here that the infamous Lord Leitrim was murdered 140 years ago. Most hostility against him was centred in Donegal, especially in Fanad where he owned 12,000 acres. Evictions were being carried out, and it was only a matter of time before a plot was hatched to assassinate him. That morning three men armed with muzzle loading guns had crossed Mulroy Bay to Rosguill by boat and were lying in wait for Lord Leitrim to pass by near Cratlagh Wood. He was on his way to Millford (a village he owned in its entirety). His assassination was considered a pivotal point in the Land League's founding the following year in 1879.

Millford (Baile na nGalloglach) at bottom of Mulroy Bay

A few miles before I reached Carrickart I decided to take a little detour down to the Blaney Bridge (now I had seen it from both sides). This scenic way into Carrickart turned out to be a narrow and hilly coastal road, but it was traffic-free and despite the heavy mist, it was a lovely way to approach and arrive at my destination and finish this weekend's adventure. I'm thankful to Brendan, the manager at Fanad Lodge, who collected me from Carrickart and drove me back to the Lodge to collect my car.

STAGE 24:

Co. Donegal: Carrickart to Creeslough

Saturday 22 Sept 2018

39.9 km or 24.8 miles

I've now completed over 1,000 km since I left Omeath, Co. Louth last year with Helen and Sean. This month I found myself in a very remote part of Donegal in the Rosguill Peninsula where apparently, the last of the O'Boyles died in 1360 before the MacSweeneys of Scotland took over. So really, I'm just reclaiming the old O'Boyle land back again! It's a damp start to the day as I leave Carrickart at 9.00 am. I can even count the nine church bells ringing in the distance as I'm leaving the village, heading north towards Island Roy. Apparently on some maps Island Roy is not even shown, and I must admit I'd never heard of it before. So I cross a small bridge and arrive on Roy (or Oileán Ruaidh, meaning 'red island' due to the rusty colour of the vegetation). I don't delay on the island, and when I get back to the mainland, I take a sharp right turn and run along a slightly rocky shore. After a while, I notice a grassy path up off the shore, which is much better for running on. I eventually come to Rosepenna pier, and I take a sharp left turn just before the pier (on a better road now), and I head north. The rain has now stopped completely. It turns out to be another beautiful day in Donegal. So far, so good but this is where it all started to go wrong! After passing the 'Singing Pub' I should have taken a right turn that would have brought me to the top of the Rossguill Peninsula. Instead I followed the road straight ahead, stopping though to admire (and take a picture of) the beautiful Tra na Rossann beach. At this stage I presumed I was still heading north but in fact I was really going west! I get talking to a man

Tra na Rossann beach, Rosguill, Donegal

and he tells me I'm only two miles north of Downings beach. This came as a bit of a shock as I thought I was very near Melmore Head at the top of Rosguill! So I arrived shortly in Downings quicker than I thought, having not covered all of Rossguill. At Downings, I followed the sign (right) for the pier and went down the wide expansive beach steps. I carried on running along the beach until it came to an end at the golf course. As I got closer to Creeslough, there were lovely views across to Doe Castle, and shortly afterwards I crossed a very picturesque bridge over the river Lackagh (An Leacach). I avoided the main road into Creeslough by following the Cycle signs (right turn towards Doe Castle). With Muckish Mountain standing tall behind it was a lovely quiet way to approach Creeslough and complete Stage 24.

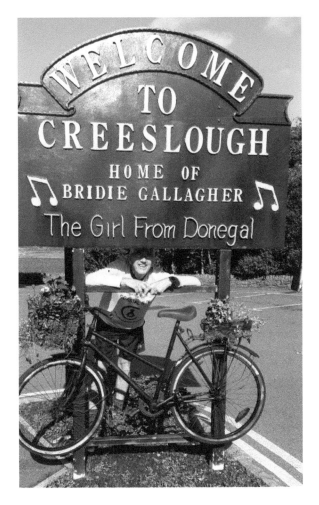

Arriving in Creeslough, Co. Donegal

Stage 24 - Revisited: Co. Donegal: Tra na Rossann to Melmore Head

Sunday 21 Oct 2018

9.6 km or 6 miles

I convinced Maureen and Brian to go back to the scene of the crime! The crime was that I had <u>not</u> completed Stage 24 properly last month. This six-mile stretch might not seem very long, but it involved climbing three hills in a remote area ...with my son Brian... and Maureen did some of it too! The day didn't start well. It rained all morning, and there was a particularly heavy shower as we left Arnolds Hotel in nearby Dunfanaghy. I wondered if Maureen and Brian would be able to tackle this walk (no I didn't expect them to run it!). Anyway we arrived at Tra na Rossann beach in Rosguill at about 11.15 am. On the positive side, I had detailed instructions about walking to Melmore Head. I had found this information sheet (on the internet) outlining the route to take (from Tra na Rossann to Melmore Head) which proved invaluable

…And so we walked along Tra na Rossann to the end of the beach (keeping the sea on our left on this occasion) and then began our climb. Our first hill, Crocknasleigh, is the highest point in Rosguill. We could clearly see the beach below us and with the sun coming out, Tory Island was stretching out in the distance. Maureen didn't quite make it to Crocknasleigh (and went back to the car), but Brian and I carry on up to the top.

Brian on Crocknasleigh – highest point in Rossguill, Co. Donegal

Brian and I follow our instructions from the sheet, making our way to the next hill. It turns out Brian is quite fit and makes it up to the second hill/peak without too much difficulty. However, getting down from this hill poses a problem. We can see Boyeeghter Strand below us, but it's quite a descent. We slowly make our way down and then have a lovely flat grassy stretch to walk on with Melmore Lough on our right hand side. We head over to Murder Hole Beach (nobody seems to know how it got its name!) Anyway, Brian is still in good form as we slide down the sand dunes onto the strand at Murder Hole.

Brian at Murder Hole beach in Rossguill, Co. Donegal

It's turned out to be another sunny day with no sign of any more rain. Brian and I find our way to the 'old derelict farmhouse' and climb our last hill, Melmore Hill and eventually come back to the large caravan park and follow the main road out of the park. I reckon Brian has done enough today – I'm so proud of him! Maureen comes to meet us at Melmore Caravan Park, and I complete the loop on my own, running back along the main road to Tra na Rossann beach. Mission accomplished – Stage 24 completed in full!

STAGE 25:

❖

Co. Donegal: Creeslough to Dunfanaghy

Saturday 20 Oct 2018

44.8 km or 27.8 miles

This month's run was another early start as Maureen and Brian drove with me to Donegal and dropped me off at Creeslough ('Home of Bridie Gallagher' as the sign with the bicycle says!). I hadn't really heard much about the singer, Bridie Gallagher but she still holds the record for the largest number of people in attendance at the Albert Hall when more than 7,500 were there to hear her perform.

With Maureen and Brian at Creeslough

I had heard of Creeslough through this song (also called "The Emigrant's Letter") which was written by the great Percy French. The idea for the song came from a remark French overheard during his voyage to Canada. One emigrant on board the ship was heard to say to his friend as they leaned over the rail of the ship: "Well Mick, they'll be cuttin' the corn in Creeslough today." (The emigrant was already homesick before he even left Ireland!)

It's a pleasant morning as I head north towards Dunfanaghy. Of course, as usual, I'm determined to stick strictly to the coast so after about 2 km I take a right turn at Clonbeg Glebe, signposted to 'Ards Friary'. I'm now in a peninsula called Ards or Ards Forest Park. I follow a quiet country road until I reach the Friary (Retreat and Conference Centre). There's a church and grotto here and a nice grassy area by the shoreline which leads on to a coastal path. I follow the coastal walk after leaving the Friary. I pass a small beach, and then I climb a wee hill, still following the path. On my right, I see a lovely secluded beach (Lucky Shell Beach). A friend of mine, Melanie, had told me about her 'secret' beach so I was glad to get someone to take a picture of me in front of it. I leave the path and head down onto Lucky Shell Beach itself and run to the far end.

Me on Lucky Shell beach, near Creeslough, Co. Donegal

Ards Forest – the Donegal Ards Peninsula!

At the end of the beach, I make my way roughly through the trees and eventually I find a forest trail that takes me onto the north side of the peninsula. On this north side, there's even more beautiful trees and beaches, and I'm beginning to feel like I'm on a tropical island. The weather even seems slightly tropical, although it's October!

In 1610 the Lord Deputy granted 2,000 acres of the peninsula to Turlough O'Boyle. The proposal was approved on certain stipulations. One was that O'Boyle would desist from involvement in any rebellion. However, as early as 1641 a rebellion erupted in Fanad and yes, the O'Boyles being the O'Boyles couldn't resist a good fight! This meant the immediate forfeiture of the land around the Ards Forest!

Still in Ards Forest, but now on the north side of the peninsula, I can clearly see the sandy shore across the bay on the next peninsula, and I'm tempted to try to cross the 'bay' (or Back Strand) which would bring me to Marble Hill strand. I realise though that the tide is coming in (low tide was about 10.30 and its midday now).

Eventually I decide to take the main road out of Ards Forest. After a while, I cross the Carrownamaddy river, and I take a sharp right turn and run along a rough path, keeping the river on my right. Some of the path had eroded away in recent storms, but I'm able to cross over.

I decide (in my wisdom!) that I should try to get down on the shore so that I can get onto the 'Back Strand'. My plan is to run along the Back Strand and follow the coastline all the way to Marble Hill strand. I struggle through some trees, but I do eventually get down on the shoreline. This is a strange shore to be running on. It's quite heavy sand and not exactly 'sand for the feet of the runner'. Still it's completely traffic (and people) free, and in this perfect weather, I have the lonely and lovely sound of the curlew to keep me company. I reckon Marble Hill Strand should be just around the corner, shouldn't it?

I would not recommend trying to get to Marble Hill beach this way – best to follow one of the minor roads rather than 'rough it' along the coast like I did. Anyway it seemed logical (at the time!) to follow the coastal route. That was until I started to notice the 'Private Property' signs as the bay opened up at Clonmass Point and Clonmass Isle!

So how can I get to Marble Hill Strand?

In the end, I had no choice, whether the owner liked it or not, but to cross over his fence. Now, from the hilltop, I could see the lovely Marble Hill strand clearly below. I decided I'd better climb back outside over the fence again and followed what I thought might be a nice cliff top walk - except there was hardly room to walk along the cliff because the fence came right out to the edge, some of it was even made of barbed wire. I slowly made my way down to Marble Hill Strand (holding onto the fence as I did!) and eventually got onto the beach - so relieved to be running on a flat surface again!

I came around this cliff - barbed wire didn't help (Marble Hill, Co. Donegal)

Time was moving on, and I still had a long way to go! I needed cheering up, and I was delighted and nicely surprised when Maureen and Brian met me on Marble Hill beach.

I definitely needed a break, and I was also thirsty and hungry. Luckily Maureen had some homemade buns in the car.

After a short break, I continued around the coast road until I come to Port Na Blaiche (port of the flowers). I kept running until I came to Dunfanaghy Golf Course and a 'Tra' sign pointing down to the beach. This was Killahoey Strand, and the sand here was more like 'sand for the feet of the runner'. I noticed that a review referred to this beach as 'a little slice of heaven' and it led all the way into the main street in Dunfanaghy. I spotted Arnolds Hotel where I knew we were staying and resisted the temptation to finish here for today! I decided that I would continue up to Horn Head. After crossing Horn Head

Bridge (just outside Dunfanaghy) I came to a junction and followed the sign Left to Horn Head, knowing that I could do a loop and return via the coast on the eastern side.

It seemed to be one long climb up to Horn Head, and at this stage I had no energy to run, but at least it was a quick vertical walk to the top. The higher I climbed, the windier it got and when I eventually reached the little concrete hut at the top, the wind was blowing from all angles.

It was windy at Horn Head (Co. Donegal)

Tory Island stood out in the distance – probably in mourning now as Patsy Dan, the King of Tory, had just died yesterday. I didn't delay too long at the top of Horn Head and started running down again, following the Wild Atlantic Way sign. It was a bit further this way, but the views over Sheephaven Bay were spectacular. It was a tough run today, and I was relieved to arrive back in Dunfanaghy and finish Stage 25.

STAGE 26:

❖

Co. Donegal: Dunfanaghy to Falcarragh

Saturday 19 Jan 2019

29.2 km or 18.2 miles

Another new year of running and I was joined on this month's coastal run by my good friend Johnny McGrath, who also lives in Bangor and is another North Down AC member. It's the first time I've had any company since crossing the Derry/Donegal border in March 2018. After completing 456 km on my own, I'm delighted to have a running partner today!

It's a wet morning as Johnny and I leave Bangor at 5.50 am, making sure we make it to Falcarragh in time for the 9.30 parkrun. The weather is slowly improving, and by the time we cross the Foyle Bridge and head towards Donegal the rain has cleared, and it's brightening up nicely.

Bridge of Tears:

Johnny and I have a lovely drive through the hills of Donegal as dawn is breaking. Just before we get to Falcarragh, as the road winds around, we cross over a small bridge. It's called the Bridge of Tears. The sign in Irish says 'family and friends of the person leaving for foreign lands would come this far'. We can imagine how sad and heartbreaking that must have been saying goodbye to someone, possibly forever, as they may never see them again.

This part of Donegal suffered even more during the Irish Famine and a workhouse was opened in Dunfanaghy in the 1840's to feed the needy. The French sociologist, de

Beaumont made a trip to Ireland at that time and *wrote "I have seen the Indian in his forests, and the Negro in his chains, and thought that I saw the very extreme of human wretchedness but an entire nation of paupers is what was never seen until it was shown in Ireland."*

Falcarragh parkrun: It was a long way to come to do a parkrun, but the welcome we got made it all worthwhile. We meet the organisers, Tom and Paul and about 100 people complete the parkrun, which is quite a big crowd for a winter's morning in north-west Donegal. It's a lovely run through a small forest and orchard. After the parkrun, we join everyone for tea and buns. Two runners, Peter and Janet, kindly drive us back to our starting point in Dunfanaghy (Fort of the Fair-Haired Warrior) for today's Coastal Run.

Johnny and I leave Dunfanaghy at 10.50 am and make our way north as far as Horn Head bridge, just about 1k outside Dunfanaghy. On this lovely sunny day we were both in good form, just as this local poet felt.

> *'I shuffled home past Horn Head bridge from collecting sticks and kindling while corncrakes rasped from Figart Ridge as summer light was dwindling'*

Immediately after crossing Horn Head Bridge, we take a left turn along a rough trail towards the sea. We follow the trail, which eventually fades away but we can see the sea in the distance and we carry on over fields and sand dunes. After about 2 km we reach the amazing Tramore Beach.

Me on Tramore Beach near Dunfanaghy, north west Donegal

I suppose I can say that I've finally reached the WEST coast of Ireland. The sun is shining, the sea is calm, and Johnny and I enjoy running on the sand (lovely 'sand for the feet of the runner'). Its low tide too, which means we have a massive beach all to ourselves with perfect views of Tory Island and also nearby Inishbofin (island of the white cow). The beach is about 3 km long and at the end there's a cliff and headland ahead which separates us from the next beach (Falcarragh strand). We climb a steep hill or two and start looking for this trail/lane we've seen on our maps. Eventually we find the lane and run along it and after a few more turns we arrive on Falcarragh beach.

Although its mid January it's not at all cold today. Remember we're 55 degrees north of the equator and on exactly the same latitude as Moscow and parts of Alaska. However the warm Gulf Stream from the Atlantic is doing its work, embracing Donegal and making it a very pleasant day.

Crossing stream on Falcarragh beach. Donegal

We run to the end of Falcarragh beach, aptly named Finlays Point (same name as Johnny's son!). We can see across the narrow passage to the Dooey peninsula which we plan to tackle later this afternoon. For now, we continue to follow the coast (keeping the sea on our right-hand side, as always!) and shortly arrive in Falcarragh. We run back to the GAA club where the parkrun started this morning and where we left our car.

Dooey/Magheroarty Peninsula:

As it was a relatively short stage today, we decide to complete this peninsula as well (it will save me about 5 miles on my next stage). We drive from the GAA club in Falcarragh and park near Tory Island Pier. (the word Tory comes from the old Irish word Tóraidhe which means bandit) As the tide is coming in now, we decide to run this peninsula clock-wise. This heavy sand is definitely not for the feet of the runner! We struggle to the end of the peninsula, looking across at Finlay's Point and Falcarragh beach where we'd been earlier. When we do turn right around the 'corner', we notice the sand is harder and much easier to make progress. We leave the beach and come to a nice coastal trail that brings us back to the carpark at Tory Island pier.

So with Stage 26 completed, Johnny and I enjoy a sunny walk to the end of Tory Pier, and afterwards we head up to Teach Coll (Colls Bar) for a well-deserved pint!

STAGE 27:

❖

Co. Donegal: Falcarragh to Bunbeg (via bloody foreland)

Saturday 9 March 2019

40.8 km or 25.3 miles

"I mind the waiting valleys that light up the dawn of day and I mind the dawn light creeping on the rugged crests of grey" (The Hills of Donegal)

I t's a wet (and cold) morning as I leave Bangor at 6.10 am. I'm on my own today, but I was confident it was going to be a straightforward run with a coastal path for most of the way. Driving through Belfast, there's already light snow coming down which continues all the way across the border.

When I get onto the snowy hills of Donegal, the mountain road across by Errigal is just about driveable, but it does mean I arrive later in Bunbeg than planned.

A majestic view of Errigal

I leave my car in Bunbeg and get a taxi to Falcarragh. I arrive at the GAA Club just as the Falcarragh parkrun is finishing. I had not planned to do the parkrun in any case, but get chatting to a man called Eddie McFadden, and I avail of a nice mug of tea and some banana bread before I start today's adventure from Falcarragh.

The name Falcarragh (literally 'the Wall Stone') has been used since 1850, as it was believed that the 'Na Crois Bhealaí', the Cross Roads, was already too common a name in Ireland.

I start my run, heading west at the Crossroads. After a few miles, I arrived at the small village of Gortahork (or Gort an Choirce) where Johnny and I had stayed when we did Stage 26 back on 17 January. Since I was here last, there was a terrible tragedy where four young men lost their lives in a car accident. On and on for another few miles along the country road and I reach the Tory Island/Inishbofin Pier. Luckily for me, I don't have to run around the Dooey/Magheroarty peninsula as Johnny and I already completed that section over the very soft sand back in January.

View of Magheroarty peninsula

It seems to be a beautiful day now, and I'm beginning to feel overdressed in my hat, gloves and leggings. Later, I'm really glad I wrapped up so much!

I'm also now in training for my first (and only) marathon in Connemara on 14 April, so I don't mind getting the mileage up today. I'm still heading west, and I pass Teach Coll (Colls Bar) where Johnny and I enjoyed a pint last time!

Muckish mountain

Suddenly the weather has changed, and the rain is coming down (this seemed to be the trend for the day, sunshine and showers!) Shortly I come to another 'Crois Bhealai' (crossroads), and I take a right (north) towards the sea, signposted as 'Sli an Earagail', and I follow this beautiful quiet coastal route all the way around the bloody foreland.

The Bloody Foreland: (Cnoc Fola):

I presumed this coastal section was called bloody foreland after some gruesome (and bloody!) battle or I thought, perhaps it might be something to do with The Spanish Armada, with boats crashing against the Atlantic cliffs but Bloody Foreland actually got its name from the evening (westerly) sun illuminating the rocks on the coast. I follow the country road until I come to a sign to the right, pointing towards 'Bloody Foreland Viewing Point'. There's a rough path here which disappears after a while, and then I find myself running on a rough grassy headland.

Inishsirrer & Inishmeane: Just across the sea, I can see two islands, about a mile off the coast. There are also a couple of islands off the west coast of Galway called Inisheer and Inishmean, but these Donegal islands are uninhabited unlike the Galway islands. Innishsirrer was once a thriving fishing community, but all that remains now is a "Ghost Town" with abandoned cottages and shops with apparently, even furniture left behind after the last residents left.

As I'm standing on the windy beach admiring the two islands, I see a lady in the distance running on the strand followed by six or seven terriers. As I restart my run, the wee dogs come rushing towards me, nipping and barking at my legs. Meanwhile the lady keeps running alone in the distance, ignoring her wayward dogs and oblivious to my shouts for them to get away!

Eventually I get moving again, and I keep running on the (now heavy and soft) sandy shore until I come to a narrow river/stream which is a bit too wide (and deep) to cross.

I hug the river as it winds inland and eventually I see a narrow spot and decide to take a running jump and cross the river. I'm soon up on the R257 again, just before the village of Derrybeg.

Gweedore/Gaoth Dobhair: I'm now in the area called Gaoth Dobhair which stretches some 26 km north to south and around 14 km east to west and is one of Europe's most densely populated rural areas. It is the largest Irish-speaking parish in Ireland with a population of over 4,000. After the Plantation of Ulster Irish-speaking families were driven from their fertile lands in the Lagan Valley and made their way to the poor boglands of west Donegal. I run on towards Derrybeg, climbing the hill at the top of the village and then taking a right down towards the Golf course. It's a long run down to the shore, but eventually I arrive at a small secluded beach. I follow the coast on another grassy headland all the way to Maherclogher beach (Bunbeg) which opens out in front of me.

Errigal peeping over horizon at Bunbeg with Baid Eddie on left

Finally, as I reach my destination at the end of the strand, I come across a wreck of a boat know as Baid Eddie (Eddie's boat). Behind it, I can see snow-capped Mount Errigal, Donegal's highest peak, peeping over the horizon. It's the perfect picture to end today's adventure.

With fellow coastal runners Rachel Winter and Simon Clark

Coasting around Ireland

It seems like there are quite a few people running (or walking) around Ireland. It's not a competition or race like Scott and Armundsen had when they were trying to reach the South Pole, but nevertheless it's interesting to compare stories. Of course Bangor's own Terry Eakin aka Herbie Herb started it all in 2013 completing the coast of N.Ireland. I referred to Terry at the start of my book. I remember Terry telling me about a man who ran/walked around Ireland years ago, and when he died, his ashes were spread on the north Antrim coast. In early 2018 Mary Hickey did her 'Lap the Map' of Ireland to aid the RNLI. I ran with Mary from Donaghadee to Belfast in January and met her again in February when she had already reached Galway. Another lady, Karen Penny ('The Penny Rolls On') has recently started her walk (around Ireland and Britain!). I hope to bump into her along the coast sometime later this year. (PS I met Karen in Dungloe after my next Run, Stage 28 and since then she's completed all of the island of Ireland)

In August (2018) Rachel Winter and Simon Clark started their own adventure in Dublin and like Karen Penny, they bucked the trend by running clockwise. They called themselves 'Two Hearts Four Feet'. They've now covered most of Ireland, raising funds for Ecologia Youth Trust and have completed over 2,000 miles. Simon and Rachel arrived in Bangor the day after my coastal run (10 March) and stayed with me for one night before heading south towards Dublin again. (PS They've since completed all of Ireland). Simon and Rachel say they also met Marty Holland (Coast for Cancer) near Limerick who walked the coast (3500 km-4000 km) in 2016/2017 and young Alex Ellis-Roswell, who walked Britain Ireland for the RNLI in 2014-17. All of these coastal runners (or walkers) have their own unique story to tell.

STAGE 28:

❖

Co. Donegal: Bunbeg to Dungloe

Saturday 30 March 2019

58.2 km or 36.1 miles

"For my part, I travel not to go anywhere, but just to go. I travel for travel's sake. The great affair is to move". Robert Louis Stevenson

Dawn is already breaking as I leave Bangor at 6.00 am. A couple of hours later, I drive through Letterkenny and enter rural Donegal. It's a dull morning but so uplifting to see those beautiful hills again. I cross over the mountain road - these hills/mountains are called the Seven Sisters and are dominated, of course, by big sister Errigal.

When I finally arrive in Bunbeg (the capital of Gweedore/Gaoth Dobhair) I leave my car at the big Healthwise Chemist in Bunbeg and take to the road once again.

I run along the quiet country road in the direction of Dungloe (or 'An Clochan Liath' in Irish) and then take a right turn towards Annagry and Donegal Airport.

I continue running north up the peninsula following the airport symbol. It's amazing to see an airport in this picturesque location. There's a small football pitch just outside the terminal building, and it looks like there's a Saturday morning under 10 training session taking place!

Donegal Airport: No surprise that the airport has just been voted the world's most scenic airport for the second year running in a survey by PrivateFly. I should mention too that

Donegal was voted the coolest place in the world to visit in 2017 by 'National Geographic Traveller'. Also, the weather is slowly improving so I think I'm in a good place this morning!

I pass the airport and run to the top of the Carrickfin peninsula, and I clearly see the islands of Inishinny (island of the fox) and the island of Gola (pronounced Gowla). PS: I did come back here a year later to see if I could reach Inishinny at low tide, but there was a strong channel of water blocking any access. Gola Island is even further out to sea and has an interesting history.

Inishinny Island and Gola behind

Gabhla/Gola Island, Spanish Armada and Robert Louis Stevenson:

I think most people who learned Irish would be very familiar with the song 'Baidin Fheidhimi (d'imigh go Gabhla). It's about a fatal drowning of a man called Felim, and the song was written by Felim's brother. I also read that the famous writer Robert Louis Stevenson stayed in Bunbeg. He was captivated by Gola and the tales of the Spanish Armada and the wreck, La Juliana, which crashed on the island of Gola. Apparently RLS was so inspired by these stories that he wrote Treasure Island. His book could have been called Gold Island or Gola Island!

I cross over to the north-west side of the Carrickfin peninsula, making sure to keep the sea on my right! However, there's no road or even track on this side. I rough it along the shore, but eventually I come over a headland to see a beautiful long beach ahead – its Carrickfin strand. Amazing to have such a lovely (blue flag) beach just beside the airport!

Imagine having a beach like this at the airport

I see an island in the distance which is called Inishfree Lower (and later I'll pass Inishfree Upper, near Burtonport). I should point out that neither of these islands is the Inishfree immortalised by WB Yeats or by John Ford! Yeat's 'Lake Island of Inishfree' is in Sligo and the Quiet Man's Inishfree is supposed to represent the island of Ireland.

After leaving Carrickfin beach, I continue along rough grassy headlands. It's sometimes muddy now, and I struggle as I climb over a few barbed wire fences. After a while, I come to a monument near Ballymanus to commemorate nineteen young men who lost their lives when a sea mine exploded in 1943. Also at nearby Mullaghderg beach down on the shore, there's a plaque to commemorate four young female students who drowned in 1972. I slowly make my way up a sandy path which leads me eventually to the village of Kincaslough.

I'm so glad to have a break (and a drink) here at the Post Office/Shop. Kincaslough, of course, is well known because it's the home of the country singer, Daniel O'Donnell. Back in the 1980s, my wife, Maureen was studying in GMIT in Galway with the famous singer. Maureen said that Daniel told their fellow students that he was dropping out of college because he wanted 'to make it big in country music'. And in fairness to him, he did!

About a mile after passing Kincaslough, I take a right turn that brings me over an old bridge onto Cruit Island. (pronounced Critch)

This time I decide to stick to the country road and I follow the windy, hilly road all the way to the Golf Course at the very top of the island. I pause briefly at the most northerly spot, looking across at Owey Island. (Owey means 'caves' and apparently there are underground caves and taverns on that island).

I retrace my steps and run back down Cruit Island. I pass a memorial dedicated to Darren Mills, and I heard that there is a 5 km Memorial Run/Walk on the island every year, which is a really lovely way to remember him.

Errigal mountain watching over me all day!

I'm definitely tiring now, and I'm beginning to wonder if I was too ambitious trying to reach Dungloe (An Clochan Liath) today. Just before I get to Keadue Strand, I see a sign saying only 7 km to Burtonport (Ailt an Chorrain), and I'm very tempted to continue on the main road.

However, I had to remind myself that this is a strict <u>coastal</u> run. Therefore, after I pass a soccer pitch at Keadue (Packy Bonner's old club!), I take a right down towards the sea. I knew there was a nice beach in this direction, and after roughing it along the coast for a while; I eventually came to a coastal path.

Somewhere in Cruit Island, west Donegal

Soon I arrive at another one of Donegal's hidden gems - another golden beach, called Cloch Ghlas. There's even a blue sky now, and Errigal is still clearly visible – the 'wee' peak has been my constant companion today!

I run along the beach to the end and follow a sandy path that eventually leads to a trail and then a narrow road. Yes, I'm glad I took the coastal route to Burtonport – even though I'm struggling now to keep my body moving!

I decide to have a break in Burtonport. I've already completed 32 miles today, and I'm getting hungry and thirsty (I've finished my Yorkie bar back on Cruit Island, and I haven't had a drink since Kincaslough)

At Burtonport (Ailt an Chorrain) the ferry from Aranmore is just arriving. I can even see the cottages on Rutland Island across the bay. In fact this area played a very significant part in the 1798 Revolution. Back then, Rutland Island with its thriving herring industry was the main commercial centre of the whole North West.

Rutland Island and Napper Tandy: In 1798 Napper Tandy took possession of the Post Office in Rutland Island, hoisted an Irish Flag and issued a proclamation (maybe the 1916 leaders were following in his footsteps when they took over Dublin's GPO!) Tandy was later tried for treason and sentenced to death, but unlike Wolf Tone, his life was spared. Napper Tandy was inspired by the French Revolution in 1789 and even had a connection and friendship with Napoleon. Apparently, after Tandy was convicted Napoleon intervened on his behalf and is even said to have made Tandy's release a condition of signing the Treaty of Amiens, an agreement signed by Britain, France, Spain and the Netherlands.

I call into the only pub in Burtonport and have a nice glass of Cidona (cider without the alcohol!) before continuing. It's tough-going over the last few miles, but I'm quietly satisfied to eventually arrive in An Clochan Liath (Dungloe) which is the capital of The Rosses and my finish line today.

Stage 28 – Revisited: OILEAN NA MARBH (the island of the dead), Carrickfin Peninsula

Saturday 5 December 2020

No extra mileage

I returned to Carrickfin and I went back with Maureen and Brian on a cold and showery December afternoon.

Brian & Maureen at low tide crossing to Oilean na Marbh

197

Although I had passed very close to this island back in March 2019 (when I did my original run) I didn't realise the significance of this place, and in any case, you needed a low tide to access this small island. The name of the island in itself indicates a sad tale, and after I read about the history behind the name of the island, the story became even more heartbreaking. This wee island was used as a type of graveyard for stillborn babies or those babies that died before they could be baptised. It is estimated that about 500 babies were buried here on the island even up to the beginning of the 20th century. It was then a cruel society, led by the strict rules of the Catholic Church, maintaining that the unbaptised could <u>not</u> be buried in consecrated grounds.

With Maureen and Brian on this winter's day, we drove passed Donegal airport and took a left turn signposted to Tra a Bhaid (the Boat Strand). We parked on the cliff just before the pier, and across the water, we could already see a Cross on the island. It was a steep and slippy climb up onto the island itself, and I couldn't help thinking that this was not a nice journey for any parent to have to take.

Remembering special souls on Oilean na Marbh

These separate burial grounds were common all over Ireland, usually in allocated spaces just outside graveyards or churches and became known as cillineachs. I remember once hearing about my own father's siblings. In 1921, he was the youngest of fourteen children, but five of his older brothers died either stillborn or just as babies. I have a vague recollection that they were buried in a separate area and perhaps also denied a proper burial. I'm old enough too to remember learning about the unbaptised and that horrible place called Limbo where 'those souls who, though not condemned to punishment, are deprived of the joy of heaven". This was really the Catholic teaching that encouraged this kind of warped morality. However I'm glad to report that now, in the modern era, the dead on Oilean na Marbh will never be forgotten. A local man, Seamus Boyle, started a campaign this century and now there is a plaque and a memorial cross to honour (and always remember) those special souls.

STAGE 29:

Co. Donegal: Dungloe to Meenacross

Friday 3rd May 2019

23.3 km or 14.4 miles

I must admit I wasn't really in the mood for running this weekend after completing the Connamarathon (my one and only ever marathon!) and picking up a heavy cold in the weeks afterwards. However, it was great to have Maureen and Brian with me and also to be joined on Saturday and Sunday by my Bangor friends, Valerie and Philip McDonough (and their dog Pip!) who were staying in Portnoo for the bank holiday weekend.

Maureen, Brian and I travelled down on Friday afternoon and arrived in west Donegal about 5.30 pm. This evening I decided I would run clockwise, keeping the sea on my left side for a change! The reasoning being that I could finish back in Dungloe where we were staying, and Maureen wouldn't have to come back to collect me later. So my starting point was at Meenacross Church, just south of Dungloe.

Leaving Meenacross, I headed straight (south) towards the coast. Two barking dogs immediately kept me on my toes, one seemed quite vicious and was tied (tightly I hoped!) by rope to his kennel. I was glad to get past and soon I was down on a remote shoreline. Before I reached a small pier, there was a rough trail to the right, heading inland that I knew would bring me up to the quiet country road known as Falcorrib Coast Road.

Met this Italian couple who were picking up rubbish near Maghery beach

I followed this road around the coast and eventually was glad to see Maghery beach (not to be confused with another Maghery beach further south near Ardara). I thought I might be able to circle the Termon peninsula, but it didn't seem possible or practical, so I ran as far as I could along the road to the top of the peninsula and just turned around again and back towards Maghery. At this stage, I rang my old boss, Keith Harvey, who I knew was staying in Dungloe. He said he would meet me along the Maghery road, so that gave me an incentive to push on. Although today was a relatively short stage (only 23 km), I struggled this evening and was so glad to reach Dungloe (An Clochan Liath) and meet Keith (and his wife Joan, who I also worked with) and later Maureen and Brian.

Mary from Dungloe:

It was always one of my favourite songs, so it means a lot to me to be actually staying in Dungloe! Apparently the original 'Mary' was Mary Gallagher. She had a boyfriend, but her parents refused to let him marry their daughter ('it was your cruel father would not let me stay here') and he emigrated to America. Mary herself also left later for New Zealand, married another man and died a few months later after giving birth. Very sad story but then all the best songs usually have a sad tale behind them.

STAGE 30:

❖

Co. Donegal: Meenacross to Dooey Point

Saturday 4th May 2019

15.5 km or 9.6 miles

Dooey Point, north of Portnoo with Valerie and Philip McDonough and Brian of course

This was another stage that I decided to do clockwise with the sea on my left. I was so glad to be joined today by Valerie and Philip McDonough and their dog, Pip. It seemed much easier to arrange to meet the McDonoughs at Dooey Point rather than Meenacross (which is a difficult place to find!). Dooey Point was such a lovely starting point on another one of Donegal's spectacular beaches on a beautiful sunny morning.

We then headed east from Dooey beach and ran along the country road. Even when we reached the N56 we were able to avail of an off-road cycle lane. We soon came to the Drom Loch Druid sign, so we headed left along the L1743 and faced a few more wee Donegal hills! After a mile or two we decided to be a bit more adventurous, so we trampled through grass and bushes and found ourselves eventually down on a wide strand. Trying to get back on the road was tricky as we realised we had a wide stream to cross. Philip did the chivalrous thing, took off his shoes and carried his wife Valerie (piggy-back style) across the stream. After crossing the stream, I followed the pair, barefoot through the water. This stretch on the strand turned out to be a kind of 'shortcut' to Meenacross even if it was rougher terrain! Soon we spotted Maureen driving towards us to tell us we only had about 1 km to go and so we arrived at the Meenacross Church having completed stage 30 of the coastal adventure.

In a previous blog, I referred to Karen Penny (The Penny Rolls On) and how she was walking around Britain and Ireland. I had been keeping in touch with Karen on Facebook and it so happened that she was also in Dungloe this weekend (she was heading north and walking clockwise, and I was heading south and anti-clockwise). We arranged to meet on the Saturday night for a chat, and it's amazing what she's achieved since arriving in Wexford in January. (By the end of 2020, she'd already raised £78 k for Alzheimer's).

The Penny Rolls On!

STAGE 31:

❖

Co. Donegal: Dooey Point to Portnoo

Sunday 5th May 2019

25.9 km or 16.1 miles

*"**Give me your tired, your poor, your huddled masses yearning to breathe free,
I lift my lamp beside the golden door.**" (This is a good excuse for me to quote the
famous lines by Emma Lazarus referring to the Statue of Liberty – see also later)*

Maureen, Brian and I had stayed in the Riverhouse hostel in Dungloe, and we drove
back this morning again to Dooey Point to meet with Valerie and Philip.

It turned out to be a wet start, but as the day went on, it brightened up. In any case, we
had all of Dooey Strand to ourselves, and we were able to run for miles on the beach and
admire the view across to Portnoo (our finish line for today.) However, gradually the sand
got softer as we turned the corner at the end of the main beach – heavy going for 'the feet
of the runner'. Eventually we were able to get up onto the quiet coast road and follow it
all the way until we could see the Gweedarra Bridge on the N56.

Gweedarra Bridge: The first bridge was built here in 1896 mainly to shorten the journey (by 7 miles) between Glenties and Dungloe and also to connect the villages in SW
Donegal. However, it was not very suitable for vehicle traffic and in 1953 a more secure
new bridge was constructed. The new bridge was considered a major engineering feat of
its time, and even today it looks very impressive.

Although we were on a busy road, we were able to run along a lower level cycle lane for the next few miles. Suddenly after leaving the cycle lane, we came to a strange appearance of the *'Statue of Liberty'* in a garden outside a house on the main road.

With Valerie at famous statue near Portnoo

We noticed the house was for sale too but not sure if the statue was included in the price! Shortly afterwards we took a right turn, leaving the N56, towards Portnoo. Valerie and Philip were getting excited now knowing we were getting close to home turf. Philip's family has been coming to Portnoo for years, and in fact Philip's grandfather was the second ever family to have a caravan at this site.

We continued towards Portnoo and Naran, passing the village of Clooney, not to be confused with the Clooney in Co. Clare ('a mile from Spancil Hill'). Soon afterwards we took a right turn at the Lake House Hotel, which got us down towards the shore and golf course. We stuck to the coast now, trying not to distract the golfers and shortly arrived at the beautiful strand at Portnoo.

Synchronized running on Portnoo Strand

When we finally reached our destination, Philip suggested we call to the coffee stand at the beach and yes we deserved our caffeine in the sunshine.

The coffee perked me up so much that I decided to tackle nearby Inis Caoil Island. As it was low tide, I couldn't resist the opportunity! Luckily for me, Maureen and Brian had just arrived on the beach at this point, and so the three of us crossed over to the island together.

I left Maureen and Brian at the ruins of St. Connells Church on the island and proceeded to run around the whole island, worrying slightly that I wouldn't make it back before the tide came in. It's hard to believe that St. Connell and others lived here as far back as the 6th Century. Those monks would have been watching out for tides too! In the end, I had plenty of time to circle the island and made my way back along the beach to the caravan park where Valerie and Philip had put on a full and wholesome lunch for us all! It was the perfect ending to the running weekend.

STAGE 32:

Co. Donegal: Portnoo to Ardara

Sunday 23 June 2019

42.3 km or 26.3 miles

"The echo of your fiddle lingers on the breath of the wind." (Inscription on *'Fiddler' statue in Ardara*)

So I started where I finished in May at the beautiful beach in Portnoo and headed west towards Dunmore Head. (Dunmore is the same name as my mother's home village in Co. Galway. My mother would think I was totally mad running around the coast!).

Following the sheep on Dunmore Hill, just west of Portnoo

I ended up having to climb Dunmore Hill. Still the views are amazing, and I'm now quite close to the island of Roaninish which I can clearly see stretching out in the sea in front of me. (I've heard there's a lovely film made about Roaninish called 'The Secret of Roan Inish') I slowly descend Dunmore Hill and soon get close to the coast again. Eventually in the distance I could see a rough rocky beach, and I spotted a trail at the end, which I knew, would bring me up to the main country road by Kiltooris Lough.

At the other end of the Lough is O'Boyles Island. I realise I'm not too far either from O'Boyles Fort (built on an island in the middle of Doon Lough) which was the scene of the murder of Conor O'Boyle, killed by a rival family member in 1530 (better not tell my son Conor about this!)

Anyway, I keep running west along this road until I came to a right turn which takes me down towards Dawros Head where I climb over a gate and head left/south, cross-country towards the coast.

Near Dawros Head -always nice to see a stile

I follow this coastline with a mixture of small coves, beaches, bog-land and lots of sheep! Soon I come to the lovely Tramore beach (yes yet another Tramore - of course 'Tramore' means big beach!) and afterwards an even bigger, longer and nicer beach, Ballinreavy strand.

Ballinreavy Strand, near Ardara

I'm thirsty and hungry at this stage – it's a long time ago since I had breakfast in Bangor (about 5.30 am) but even more urgently I need a drink – I'm so thirsty now! I realise its 2.00 and the Ulster Football Final had just kicked off (Donegal beat Cavan, I hear later!) so another reason why there's nobody about today!

After leaving Ballinreavy beach, there's a lovely path through sand dunes. I'm running along here when I spot two couples walking. I stop to ask them for a drink and almost devour their supply. One of the men seems to recognise me, and it turns out that I had met him briefly in Portnoo when I was there in May. He is Philip McDonough's brother! Remember Philip and his wife Valerie ran with me during Stages 30 and 31. These things only happen in Ireland, where everyone knows someone who knows you!

I continue along the dunes and realise now that I'm running in an area called Sheskin-more, which is one of the most important Nature Reserves in Ireland. I eventually get down on the shore again as the tide is almost at its lowest, but I made the mistake of following the coast too far and missed the country lane up from the beach just before Ardara. I ended up tramping through a muddy beach and fields. Finally I arrive on the country lane about 3 km NW from Ardara and slowly make my way into the village, exhausted after today's run!

Ardara is indeed a nice place and was voted best village to live in 2012 by the Irish Times. There's a lovely little statue in the centre of the town dedicated to a fiddler, called John Doherty who was a Donegal fiddler from a long line of travelling tinsmiths, horse traders and musicians.

John the fiddler welcomed me to Ardara

That evening Maureen, Brian and I went to visit Maureen's cousins (Cathal and Sarah) who live nearby. On the way to their house this evening, we spotted three or four small bonfires. Its St. John's Night – 23rd June and lighting wee fires is an old Irish custom that's still remembered in this part of Donegal. Cathal and Sarah serve up a beautiful pasta dinner, and we have a wonderful evening. The expression 'eating you out of house and home' was never so apt this evening as I tucked into all four courses! We runners like to call it 'refuelling'!

Ardara to end of peninsula at Loughros Point (Part B of Stage 32)

Monday 24 June 2019: I'm not calling this a proper stage as it was only a wee run out to Loughros Point (about 9 km) which is the most westerly point from Ardara. Maureen agreed that she would meet me at the slipway at Loughros Point when I finished. I did contemplate trying to 'rough it' again along the shore, but it didn't look achievable. Also, there didn't seem to be much point in running back the same road again so I agreed (with myself!) it would be a one way run to the end of the peninsula!

As I got into Loughros peninsula, there were beautiful views south across Maghera Strand to the cliffs on the other side (it's going to be hilly on the next stage!) At one point I could even see in the distance the spectacular Assarnacally Waterfall across the wide strand - something else to look forward to on Stage 33.

Looking across to Maghera Strand from Loughros peninsula

Toward the end of the peninsula, there was a junction. A sign pointed right to Tra/Strand and left to the Slipway where I had arranged to meet Maureen and Brian.

At Loughros Point, SW Donegal

At the pier, I convinced Maureen and Brian to climb the grassy hill to the very top of the hill at Loughros Point. There we spotted letters marked by rocks on the grass, spelling out the word EIRE. I had seen similar markings at Malin Head and Melmore Point, and these have been here since World War 2 to indicate that the Republic of Ireland was a neutral country.

Today Maureen, Brian and I have this magnificent view all to ourselves with the hills of Donegal stretching out in all directions and shrouded cliffs across the bay at Maghera Strand. Even the great Atlantic Ocean to our west is today, still and peaceful.

STAGE 33:

Co. Donegal: Ardara to Glencolmcille

Friday 26 July 2019

31.5 km or 19.5 miles

"Look down on Glencolmcille, its mountain, sea and shore and wonder at such beauty that nature has allowed" (from a Destiny of Dreams by Marion McGuire)

It was like a festival of running this weekend; yes, hard work over three days (Stages 33, 34 and 35) but so enjoyable. I was delighted to be reunited with Sean and Helen, Sean for all three stages and Helen for the toughest day (climb over Slieve League) on the Saturday and for some of the run on Sunday.

At least the trip from Bangor was different this time as I'm now in SW Donegal. I passed through places in Fermanagh (Kesh and Pettico) that I'd never been to before. I had Sean for company (and navigation) today (Friday) which shortened the journey. No injury worries now and in fact earlier this month I won two M60 (male over 60) trophies in Co. Down (Portaferry 10 mile race and Crawfordsburn 5 km) and I'm 61 today!

It was just about 2.00 pm when Sean and I started our run from Ardara, heading south first, as far at the turn signposted for Maghera Beach or An Machaire (making sure not to take the Glengesh road which would bring us too far inland!). The first few miles of our run were relatively flat with a lovely view over Maghera Strand and across to Loughros peninsula. We then had a brief stop at the Assarnacally Waterfall after 8 km and got chatting to a Berlin couple and their wee girl.

Our run (or climb) only really began in earnest after we left the waterfall. We saw the sign, pointing down towards Maghera Beach and Caves but realised they were inaccessible as it was now high tide. So instead, Sean and I put our heads down to tackle the incline ahead. When we finally reached the top of the hill, we left the country road and took a right turn over a gate to join a rough trail (as per the Ordnance survey map). However, it wasn't long before the trail seemed to disappear and we were trampling through a bog.

Sean following the Glen River to Glencolmcille

It was a little bit easier when we came to the Glen River, but again there was no proper trail along by the river. We were so glad to get out the other side and pick up speed on a country road which brought us all the way down to that beautiful secluded spot on the coast called Port (or 'Pert' as the locals seem to pronounce it!)

There was another German couple to welcome us at Port (this time from Koln) even offering us some food. I was glad to take an apple from them before Sean, and I tackled the steep trail heading south (Glencolmcille Loop).

I had read about Port being an abandoned Famine village, and we could indeed see the deserted village behind us as we climbed the hill. As Sean and I ran (and walked) up the trail, I couldn't get the image of young barefooted families trampling this same trail over 180 years ago. This trail eventually led us down the hill to today's destination, Glencolmcille.

This goat welcomed Sean and I to Glencolmcille

Glencolmcille played a big part in developing Christianity in Ireland, and it was local man, Columba (521-597) who established a monastery here and gave his name to the glen. Another more recent hero of Glencolmcille is Fr. McDyer, who helped build a canning factory, craft shops and the famous folk village and museum. We were most impressed with Ireland's magnificent 'Stone Map' where stone from every county in Ireland was used in building the structure. I think Sean and I were looking forward to having a nice meal after our tough runs and climbs today. In the end we settled for tasty fish and chips which we bought from a van in Glencolmcille. We then sat in the evening sunshine for a couple of hours, outside a pub and chatting to various people. It didn't seem long before Helen and Neill arrived in their car, and we all made our way to Malin Beg Hostel where we were booked in for two nights.

Deserved pints in Glencolmcille!

After a quick shower in the hostel, we all sat around a nice fire. When someone asked Frank the owner of the hostel, *'Is there Wi-Fi here'*, he replied *'No we talk here'*, and so we did talk, chatting to other residents and enjoying a few glasses of wine around the fire. To cap it all, Helen brought along a cake she'd made. Yes, definitely one of the most enjoyable birthdays of my 61 years!

STAGE 34

Co. Donegal: Glencolmcille to Teelin (via Malinbeg and Slieve League)

Saturday 27 July 2019

26.6 km or 16.5 miles

It was an early enough start today at Malinbeg Hostel. We had to pick my car up, which was in Ardara (since yesterday), so we decided to go on a bit further north to Portnoo beach and do the new parkrun there. In any case, we had to collect Valerie McDonough who was staying the weekend at her caravan in Portnoo and who was joining us on to-day's run.

It was a beautiful morning when we arrived in Portnoo and running a parkrun on the beach (Narin Strand) was a great way to start the day. There was such a lovely friendly holiday atmosphere. Afterwards Valerie and Philip invited us back to their caravan for breakfast (wheaten bread and banana bread). We appreciated this as we had a long day ahead!

Tipperary girl, Valerie in Glencolmcille, pointing out her county

By the time we got back to Glencolmcille (to begin Stage 34) it was almost noon. There were five of us today (Helen, Neill, Valerie, Sean and me) on our own 'Mountain of Adventure'! It was a nice 10 km run before we reached Malinbeg, although Helen pointed out that it wasn't all downhill to Malinbeg (as I had mentioned!). We were glad to stop at at our hostel and have some drinks there before we tackled the high cliffs of Slieve League.

Frank, the proprietor, at the hostel advised us to take a left at the crossroads and then the first right. (PS Thanks Frank too for Clifton donation!) The small boreen turned to a trail, but it was easy enough terrain to run or walk on even when the path disappeared.

The weather was in our favour today; dry and sunny with hardly a puff of wind. Over the last few weeks, I had thought so much about this stage (and even worried about the safety aspect of it), and now I knew everything would be ok!

At Silver Strand near Malinbeg

We had marvelous views from the beginning, first looking down on Silver Strand beach and later views all over Donegal from the spectacular Cliffs of Slieve League. These cliffs are not as famous as the Cliffs of Moher, but they are three times higher and much more spectacular. It was a tough ascent, and the legs were tired after yesterday - not to mention the 15 km we already ran this morning since we left Glencolmcille! Still we kept climbing and climbing, over a few false summits and finally we reached the top, 600 metres above sea level! Strava recorded this as my steepest ever climb (256 metres ascent in just one kilometre!). On such a calm day we were so glad to feel that nice breeze when we got to the top – reminds me of how Johnny Cash describes that light Irish wind, a 'breeze is sweet as Shalimar'.

At the very top of Slieve League (600 metres high)

Tackling Slieve League from this side is truly amazing. We only met two people along the way and the best was still yet to come. The famous *'One Man's Pass'* was now stretching out in front of us. It was quite safe to walk (or run) along this narrow ridge on the top of Donegal on a day like today.

Running along 'One Man's Pass' at the top of on Slieve League

We deserved a rest after tackling Slieve League from the west side

We began to meet a few more people, and we could even run again now… well some of the way. It was still a long way down, but we were able to stick to the coast and eventually the coastal path led us all the way to the village of Teelin. At Teelin, we took a right turn and ran the 2 km down to the end of the pier, looking across at Kilcar on the other side. Apparently Teelin was one of the first settlements in Ireland, as it was a very important port in days gone by. We left the pier and retraced our steps back to the Rusty Mackerel pub. Valerie's husband Philip and dog Pip were there to greet us. Drinks and food followed, and we sat around and chatted in the evening sunshine. It was the perfect ending to a perfect day!

STAGE 35:

❖

Co. Donegal: Teelin to Killybegs

Sunday 28 July 2019

26 km or 16.2 miles

Leaving Rusty Mackerel again!

We weren't as lucky with the weather today, although it didn't rain properly until we were almost in Killybegs. Helen and Neill joined us for some of the way and turned back just before we got to Kilcar. We started at the Rusty Mackerel at Teelin running north as far as Carrick and then south along the other side of the bay. I think there might have been an opportunity to cross the river earlier (before Carrick), but we weren't confident about that.

It usually takes Sean a while to get going in the mornings and as Helen, and I powered on (and Neill sprinted miles ahead) we somehow 'lost' Sean not long after we left Carrick. As Helen recited later 'he took the high road, and we took the low road'. Eventually I was reunited with Sean at Kilcar just before the Gaelic pitches (home to the famous McHughs and McBreartys). At Kilcar, we made a sharp right turn on the main street to stay by the coast.

And so, we said goodbye to Helen and Neill who made their way back to Teelin. Meanwhile Sean and I then tackled the steep coastal road. At the top, we had perfect views back to Sleeve League and ahead to St. Johns Point. Sean and I decided then to run out the 2 km country road to the peninsula as far as Muckross Point.

On the way back from Muckross Point, we saw a sign 'Memory Lane' outside a house. The sign said, *'Call in for the craic'*, and so we did! At the back of the house, there was a lovely little tearoom with a half door. A young lady called Laura greeted us.

Laura outside 'Memory Lane' Cafe

Laura's grandfather's cart - over 200 years old!

The small tearoom had beautiful little ornaments, an old school desk and a lovely fireplace. Over the fireplace was a picture of an elderly lady. Laura explained that this was her grandmother, Annie Murphy who died recently. It was her grandmother's dream to have a little tearoom to welcome visitors. Sean and I enjoyed our tea and fruit cake. It was the perfect place to stop as we were more than half-way into today's run.

Afterwards we were still able to continue along the quiet country road for another few miles, but eventually we did have to come out onto the main road. Still the road sign said only 7 km to Killybegs. We had to be careful along this busy, windy road. Also, the rain started, but this didn't deter Sean who was now getting his second wind! Strava recorded our kilometre no. 80 and 82 (out of a total of 85 km over the whole weekend) as the fastest two at 4.48 and 4.46 minutes per km.

As we were making our way down to the harbour to finish today's run, these song words song were going through my head *'the boys of Killybegs are rolling home'*.

STAGE 36:

❖

Co. Donegal: Killybegs to St. John's Point

Sunday 25 August 2019

35.4 km or 22 miles

Donegal remembers: 1300 young men lost their lives on La Girona alone

For practical reasons I did Stage 37 yesterday, and today I've got two companions (Maureen and Brian) joining me (walking) for the first few miles. At the roundabout on the west side of Killybegs we take a road to Glenlee and do a loop via Portnacross Pier and back to the fishing harbour again.

At Portnacross Pier, SW of Killybegs

When we get back to Killybegs I say goodbye to Maureen and Brian and continue running along the harbour. It's the largest fishing port in Ireland – and when I get to the end I leave the R263 and take a right (and right again) sticking by the coast on the other side of the bay until the road comes to an end!

Outside a house, there is a family (or families) enjoying the sunshine and I stop to ask whether I can get down to the bottom of the peninsula. I get talking to Eddie McHugh, whose uncle owns the land in this area. Eddie decides to run with me the short distance to the bottom of the peninsula, and soon we're joined by his children/nieces. Here, there was such a lovely view across to Carntullagh Head with the Lighthouse on Rotten Island clearly visible.

With McHugh children at Carntullagh Head near Killybegs

William Steig, the children's author, wrote that Rotten Island is a '*horrible place filled with horrible monsters that slither, creep and crawl*'. I don't think he realised there was a real place called Rotten Island in this beautiful part of Donegal!

I continue up along the other side of the peninsula, taking a right turn at the top, and I was able to stay on a country road all the way. I ended up running through someone's garden before coming back onto the main road (N56) which I only had to stay on for 1 km until I saw the sign pointing right to St. John's Point. It's a long 7 miles to the lighthouse at the end of this narrow peninsula that seems to stretch out into the sea. I was glad to have a wee break near the end at Killultan beach where Maureen and Brian were there to greet me. The water looked tempting for me after my long run - no surprise that swimmers were making the most of it in that perfect clear blue sea.

As I was chatting to Maureen and Brian, a young female runner came by and she (Niamh McKenna) joined me on the last mile of my coastal run.

STAGE 37:

❖

Co. Donegal: St. John's Point to Donegal Town

Saturday 24 August 2019

44.3 km or 27.5 miles

Yes I did Stage 37 today on Saturday (and Stage 36 on Sunday) for practical reasons. There was light rain falling as I begin today's run at St. John's Point Lighthouse (built in 1833 to protect boats coming into Killybegs harbour). At the end of the peninsula, this area has a great reputation for deep-sea diving – the best in Ireland apparently – and we notice brave divers getting kitted out for their underwater adventure. I'm glad I'm only running!

I'm rarin' to go, and I run the first 10 km along the peninsula at a good pace. Strava tells me I'm the second fastest runner from the Lighthouse to Castle Murray at a time of 44.18. In hindsight, I'm going too fast!

I run through the village of Dunkineely, and after a mile I take a right turn along a rough track. The ordnance survey map marks this as a *'dismantled railway'*, and it does feel like that. After about 2 km I was surprised that the track brought me back out onto the main road (I think I could have stayed on the coast). After passing Inver PO, I took a right turn (really into Inver village or Inver Bar). Unfortunately the river (Eany) was much too wide to cross so I had to go back on the main road and cross the only bridge on the Eany River.

River Eany in Inver, near Donegal town

On the other side of the river I roughed it along the shore towards the bottom of the peninsula. I then climbed onto the headland, dipping under one or two electric fences along the way! I could see two farmers in the distance, and as I got closer, I stopped and told them what I was doing. They were very friendly (the Scott brothers) and it was only when I left their field and climbed over their gate that I noticed the 'beware of the bull' sign!

I was now on the country road again heading NE towards Mountcharles. I took the second turn right to try to stay by the coast, and as I came over a hill, a dog came barking towards me and wouldn't let me pass. The only human who appeared was a young girl about 3 years old.

Stopping at Salthill Co. Donegal

I waited for about ten minutes for an adult to appear (or for the dog to stop barking). In the end I had to backtrack up the hill again and continue along the main country road. I soon came to an area called Salthill. Mountcharles was originally called 'Tamhnach an Tsalainn', the 'green fields of salt'. It was strange seeing another Salthill as I grew up near the Galway Salthill!

Even though I was tiring, I eventually came onto the N56 that brought me into Donegal town. Feeling exhausted, I headed for the Abbey Hotel where Maureen and Brian were meeting me. It was my longest coastal run for a while, and I felt it!

STAGE 38:

❖

Donegal Town to Rossnowlagh

Friday 13 Sept 2019

26.9 km or 16.7 miles

I started my run from Donegal Town at 5.20 pm, confident enough that I'd arrive in Rossnowlagh a few hours later, before dark and be reunited with Maureen and Brian. However, as I've realised on this adventure, nothing goes according to plan, especially on Friday the 13th!

Brian gives me thumbs up as I leave Donegal Town

I head south along the R267, and when the footpath ends I take a right turn towards Dungally Strand, although there's no sign of any strand here! Eventually I arrive at a causeway that leads to St. Ernan's Island. Yet another island I've been to without getting on a boat! Apparently the causeway to St. Ernan's island was built in the 1800s by local workers as a gesture of gratitude to the compassionate landlord John Hamilton, whose original house still dominates the small island.

I leave the island and shortly rejoin the R267 again. At Laghy I take a right along the NW Cycle Trail and I get a nice surprise when I finally reach the shore. There's a pub (The Salmon Inn) here, and people are sitting outside enjoying the sunny evening.

A pub on the coast - an unexpected pleasure – near Donegal town!

I'm able to continue running along the coast, through the trail at Murvagh House (owner doesn't mind I was told) and then I keep left along the track until I come to a humpback bridge which leads me to a wee crossroads (signposted Donegal Golf club). At the Club House, I keep to the right and run along the edge of the golf course heading north towards the very top of the peninsula. I discover later that this is one of Ireland's longest golf courses and it does feel like it! Eventually I reach the northern shore and turn left (keeping the sea on my right as always!) Its 8.00 pm now, there's a beautiful sunset, and I reckon I've still got another good half hour to reach Rossnowlagh before it gets dark.

The ordnance map seems to show a nice long yellow stretch along the strand to Rossnowlagh but I soon realise that the beach is getting narrower as I get further south. Soon I have no sand to run on, and I'm stumbling over a rocky shoreline in the twilight. I knew high tide was at 6.30 pm, which doesn't help my situation.

Now it's getting dark! It gets to a point where I have to make a decision to leave the rocky shore and try to get onto a road. Eventually I do find a quiet country road, which turns inland and I run along it for a couple of miles. A dog comes barking out of a house but there's nobody around. I see a house with a light on, and I ring the bell a few times, to ask directions, but no one appears. Its pitch dark and I'm beginning to think this whole coastal run is a really mad idea! I stop a car to ask directions and get chatting to a friendly couple telling them my story. I think they feel a bit sorry for me and end up driving me all the way back to the guesthouse in Rossnowlagh. Thank you Betty and Denis Kelly!

STAGE 39:

❖

Co. Donegal: Rossnowlagh to Ballyshannon

Saturday 14 Sept 2019

22.3 km or 13.9 miles

After yesterday evening's disaster of a run, it was so nice to wake up to a beautiful morning and to be overlooking Rossnowlagh beach. Maureen, Brian and I were so lucky to have such lovely accommodation at the Gaslight Inn and a room with an amazing view!

My son Brian in our 'room with a view' of Rossnowlagh beach

However, even with the sun shining, I still wasn't in a mood for much running after yesterday's problems. I re-learned a lesson though about tides and how it's much easier running at low tide and in the daylight of course! I knew I had to go back and do the bit of the run I missed last night! With high tide at 7.00 am this morning I didn't mind waiting a few hours to start today's run. Also, as I missed dinner last night (just crisps and buns), I decided I needed a good breakfast before picking up where I left off last night. So after some tasty poached eggs and toast, Maureen and Brian joined me as I left the Gaslight Inn at 10.45 am.

At Rossnowlagh beach – a nice way to keep memories alive

The three of us walked along the beach at Rossnowlagh (called Belall Strand) and then took the main road up from the beach towards Manor House Holiday Park. At the Holiday Park, we were able to join the beach just about 3 km north of Rossnowlagh, and so I was able to complete the piece I missed last night!

It's now such a beautiful morning, and I see Rossnowlagh in all its glory - home to surfers, swimmers and walkers. There are magnificent views across on one side to St John's Point, Slieve League and the Donegal Hills and on the other side, Ben Bulben is clearly visible.

I say goodbye to Maureen and Brian and begin running on ahead. At the end of Rossnow-lagh beach, I rejoin the coastal road where our hotel (Gaslight Inn) is and follow this road towards Ballyshannon. After about 3 km at a small crossroads, I take a right turn towards Creevy Pier (or Bunatrahan Pier). At the pier I decide to continue running on the head-land to see can I get to Ballyshannon this way and I'm very pleasantly surprised to find a grassy path with lots of styles along the way. This is called the Creevy Coastal Walk, and it's probably the best coastal path I've been on in all my time in Donegal.

The style of Annette on the excellent Creevy Coastal Path

The views across to Sligo are spectacular too and even when the path comes to an end I can get down onto Wardtown Strand. It's such a lovely run along here and strange that I don't even meet one person on a beautiful Saturday afternoon in mid September. I have a lone curlew to keep me company though and that lovely haunting sound - not sure if it's the same curlew that's following me every month! It's low tide too, so unlike yesterday, everything is going my way! As I get closer to Ballyshannon, I realise there's a lane that I can take up towards the town, passing the cemetery on the way.

With Rory Gallagher in his home town, Ballyshannon

Then it's just a short 1 km run into the town centre to my finish line today at Rory Gallagher's statue, Ballyshannon's most famous son. Apparently when Jimi Hendrix was asked
how it felt to be the world's greatest guitarist, he is reported to have said, ***"I don't know,
go ask Rory Gallagher"***

STAGE 40:

❖

Co. Donegal: Ballyshannon to Bundoran (and finally to the Connacht/Leitrim border)

Sunday 15 Sept 2019

17.3 km or 10.7 miles

I enjoyed another hearty breakfast in the Gaslight Inn at Rossnowlagh before we checked out. It turned out to be a miserable wet morning after the fine weather over the last two days. Also my upper back has been sore all weekend, and I'm beginning to feel my age today!

Maureen drove me back to Rory Gallagher's statue in Ballyshannon to start my final Ulster stage. I knew I had to run along the R267 for about 5 km – no chance of trying to look for a coastal path this time because this part of the coast was closed off. It's Department of Defence Property occupied by the Irish Army (Finner Army Camp).

Finner Camp

Back in the troubled days of 1969, there was talk of the Irish Army preparing to cross the border (presumably from here at Finner Camp) and 'liberate' Catholic-dominated towns like Newry and Derry. Apparently plans were even drawn up by the Irish Army envisaged a series of guerrilla attacks on vital installations in Belfast.

Today it wasn't too unpleasant running on this road, and the rain was easing off as I got closer to Bundoran. Just before I got into the town, I took a right turn, signposted for

239

Tullan Strand. I ran down to the car park at the clifftop overlooking the beach and Maureen and Brian were there to meet me. I carried on my own down onto Tullan Strand – of course I couldn't resist a beautiful beach like that and as I keep saying 'sand is for the feet of the runner'!

Tullan Strand, just north of Bundoran

There were signs on Tullan Strand saying that it was unsafe for swimming because of rip tides. Also the Irish Army had 'No Entry' signs on the sand dunes as they occupied the land east of the beach.

Still the rain has stopped, and at the northern tip of the beach I'm able to run on the grassy section (hoping I'm off the military land by now!) I follow hoof prints that circled the top of the strand, and I run all the way back around the sandy beach and back to the car park. There I was able to follow a coastal path into Bundoran town. In fact, except for about 200 metres running along the main street, I was able to stay along the cliff top and run 'around' the town. When I finally reached the end of the cliff path and came inland, I was almost at the roundabout on the west side of Bundoran.

At the Donegal (Ulster)/Leitrim (Connacht) Border

On the other side of that roundabout, Maureen and Brian had parked the car and were there to greet me as I arrived. As I got closer to them, I could clearly see a sign saying *'Welcome to Leitrim'* ...and so I knew I had finally conquered the whole coast of Ulster!

It was hard to believe that I'd run around all of the coast of Ulster, all 1,590 km (or 988 miles). It was just so nice to have Maureen and Brian there at the finish. So, what started as a mad idea, to run around the coast of Co. Down, escalated into a three-year project that ended up running around all of Ulster (counties Down, Antrim, Derry and Donegal). There were a few scary moments in my adventure, some strange encounters, all kinds of extreme weather and a few wrong turns along the way. I pushed my body to the limit so many times, struggled and suffered from injuries on many occasions but eventually (that one word that doesn't really explain all the pain and worry!) I made it to the finish line!

Epilogue

---- ❖ ----

Hopefully you enjoyed reading this book, and maybe it's inspired you a little. I think we all have an adventure inside us and it doesn't have to involve anything too extreme or strenuous. To start your adventure, you don't need to give up your day-job or wait until you retire! Yes, it takes a lot of hard work, sacrificing and suffering, and you need to be realistic but also ambitious as to what you can achieve. Remember it all starts with just a mad idea!

And my mad idea is continuing! Sometimes when you read a good book and finish that last chapter, you wonder what happened next! Well now you have a chance to find out by following the Clifton Coastal Run through my blog below.

........so after completing the Ulster coast in September 2019, I took a winter break and then continued running into the province of Connacht. The fact that I was born and reared in Galway made it easy for me to tackle my native province. In February / March 2020, I was able to run around the coasts of Leitrim and Sligo before any restrictions or lockdown. A few months later, I was allowed to continue again (August/September 2020) into North West Mayo. Then we had the second lockdown and I had to take an even longer break until June 2021. I'm determined to keep running around the rest of Ireland. I can't stop now, can I? It's been such a journey so far and not knowing what's around the next corner, is always part of the whole adventure!

See my blog for my progress after I left Donegal – more hills to climb, more amazing places to see, more stories to tell – and of course some more spectacular beaches to run on. And as I keep saying, 'Sand is for the feet of the Runner'. The adventure continues!

https://cliftoncoastalrun.blogspot.com